Study Guide
for
Technical
Analysis
Explained

Study Guide for Technical Analysis Explained

Martin J. Pring

McGraw-Hill
New York Chicago San Francisco
Lisbon London Madrid Mexico City Milan
New Delhi San Juan Seoul Singapore
Sydney Toronto

McGraw-Hill

A Division of The McGraw-Hill Companies

Copyright ©2002 by McGraw-Hill. All rights reserved. Printed in the United States of America. Except as permitted under the United States Copyright Act of 1976, no part of this publication may be reproduced or distributed in any form or by any means, or stored in a data base or retrieval system, without the prior written permission of the publisher.

1 2 3 4 5 6 7 8 9 0   DOC/DOC   0 8 7 6 5 4 3 2

ISBN: 0-07-138192-9

The sponsoring editor for this book was Stephen Isaacs and the production supervisor was Clare Stanley. It was set in New Baskerville by MacAllister Publishing Services, LLC.

Printed and bound by R. R. Donnelley & Sons Company.

McGraw-Hill books are available at special quantity discounts to use as premiums and sales promotions, or for use in corporate training programs. For more information, please write to the Director of Special Sales, Professional Publishing, McGraw-Hill, Two Penn Plaza, New York, NY 10121-2298. Or contact your local bookstore.

 This book is printed on recycled, acid-free paper containing a minimum of 50% recycled de-inked fiber.

Contents

Study Guide
for
Technical
Analysis
Explained

How to Use
This Study Guide

This study guide has been designed as an adjunct to the fourth edition of *Technical Analysis Explained*. The questions are presented in several forms: multiple choice, matching answers, and fill-in-the-blanks. Since technical analysis is a visual art, concerned with chart interpretation, questions featuring charts have been included as much as possible. The book has been split into two parts: one for the questions and the other for the answers. Where necessary, the answers contain a narrative by way of explanation. In order to expedite the testing process, a series of sheets have been included at the back of the book: one set is for questions and the other as a quick reference for the answers. These sheets have been perforated for easy detachment. Even so, the reader is still encouraged to refer to those answers that contain explanations in the Answer section of the book. Some of the sheets ask you to "refer to the chart." This is because some charts require interactive action by the reader. The answer is therefore visual and cannot be clearly defined as with a letter for a multiple-choice question or a word required in blank-filling questions. Some questions ask for blanks to be filled in. In most cases, the first letter of the answer is printed in order to give you some guidance.

Each chapter of *Technical Analysis Explained*, with the exceptions of Chapter 17, "Putting the Indicators Together," and Chapter 28, "Checkpoints for Identifying Primary Stock Market Peaks and Troughs," has been allocated a quiz. Their sizes vary, depending upon the length of material contained in the book.

Readers are advised to first study the relevant chapters in *Technical Analysis Explained* and then proceed to the testing phase. A brief summary of the subject matter contained in each individual quiz is included at the beginning of each *Study Guide* chapter. This is a partial list of the more important subjects covered by the quiz and is included as a guide. By making a more careful study of these topics, the reader will be in a better position to answer the various questions more accurately.

If less than 70 percent of the questions are answered correctly, it is suggested that further study take place. This should not be done right away. A
better approach is to read through more chapters and come back at a later
date to the problem chapter or chapters. In this way there will be less of a
tendency to cram or force the learning process, but to let it evolve in a more
leisurely and thoughtful way.

1
The Market Cycle Model

Questions

Subjects to Be Covered

The most common types of trends
The basics of peak-and-trough analysis
How peaks and troughs are recognized

1. Name the three most important trends:
   A. _____
   B. _____
   C. _____

2. Match the answers for the duration of these trends:
   A. Short   _____   A. 10 to 25 years
   B. Intermediate   _____   B. 2 to 6 weeks
   C. Primary   _____   C. 6 weeks to 9 months
   D. Secular   _____   D. 1 to 2 years

3. Who needs to have an understanding of the direction and maturity of the main trend?
   A. Investors
   B. Traders
   C. A and B
   D. None of the above

4. Peak-and-trough analysis _____.
   A. Is far too simplistic an approach for technicians to deal with
   B. Was very useful in Dow's day but is now outdated by more
      sophisticated approaches and tools
   C. Should be used in conjunction with other tools in the weight of
      the evidence approach
   D. Only works with short and intermediate trends
   E. C and D

5. In the following chart, which letter marks the reversal in the upward
   progression of troughs?
   A. _____
   B. _____
   C. _____
   D. _____

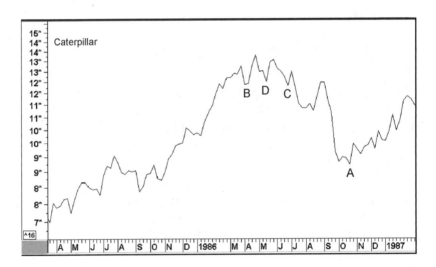

6. Can the principles of peak-and-trough progression be applied to a
   5-minute bar chart?
   A. Yes
   B. No

7. In a general sense, why are longer-term trends easier to spot?
   A. Because the bigger they are, the easier it is to see them.
   B. Because there is less random noise the longer the trend. Also, the
      expectations of market participants tend to unfold in a more
      gradual way as the fundamentals evolve.

C. Because there are always five intermediate movements in every primary trend so all you have to do is count to five.

D. None of the above.

8. Please look at the following chart featuring Citigroup. If you knew that the high and low preceding the rally at point A were 6 and 4, respectively, and the close at A was 4.25, would this represent a legitimate peak in peak-and-trough analysis?

A. Yes

B. No

9. The series of declining peaks and troughs in the following Citigroup chart is reversed at point_____.

A.

B.

C.

D.

E.

F. None of the above

10. At point B in the chart featuring Citigroup, the series of rising peaks and troughs was reversed.

A. True

B. False

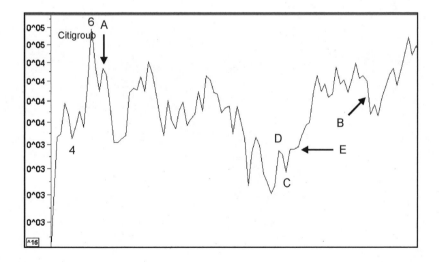

1
The Market Cycle Model

Answers

1. **Short, intermediate, and primary.** Any order qualifies as a correct answer.

2. **A = B; B = C; C = D; D = A.**

3. **C.** Investors need to know the direction of the long-term trend to correctly position themselves for the long term. Since short-term contratrend moves often result in weak price movements and numerous whipsaws, short-term traders also need to form an opinion on the direction of the primary trend. A well-known trading rule is, "Always trade in the direction of the trend."

4. **C.** Peak-and-trough analysis is a basic tool of technical analysis and should never be underrated.

5. **C.**

6. **A.** The principles of technical analysis can be applied to any security in any time frame.

7. **B.** Not only are they easier to spot, but generally speaking, the longer the time span, the more accurate the indicator.

8. B. No, the rally at point A did not retrace between one-third and two-thirds of the previous decline.

9. E. This is because the series of declining troughs was still intact at point D.

10. B. Only the series of rising troughs was reversed at B; the rising peaks were still intact.

2

The Relationship Between the Financial Markets and the Business Cycle

Questions

Subjects to Be Covered

The chronological relationship between the financial markets and the
business cycle
When they peak and trough in the cycle
Understanding the significance of the leads and lags
The six stages
Double cycles
The role of technical analysis

1. Trends in financial markets are _____.
   A. Determined by investors' expectations of movements in the
   economy
   B. The effect those changes are likely to have on the price of the
   asset in which a specific financial market deals
   C. The psychological attitude of investors to these fundamental
   factors
   D. All of the above

2. Which is the correct chronological sequence for peaks and troughs in the financial markets over the course of the business cycle?
  A. Bonds, stocks, commodities
  B. Stocks, commodities, bonds
  C. Bonds, gold stocks, commodities
  D. None of the above

3. When are commodities most likely to bottom during a recession?
  A. When it is particularly severe
  B. When the preceding commodity rally has been particularly speculative
  C. When stocks bottom earlier than usual
  D. Never

4. Why do bonds, stocks, and commodities experience moves of different magnitude and duration in different cycles?
  A. Because they discount different things
  B. Because each business cycle has different characteristics
  C. Because the leads and lags differ
  D. Because of the normal business cycle chronological sequence

5. If there is no recession, there is no financial market cycle.
  A. True
  B. False

6. If the lead between bonds and stocks at a market bottom is particularly long, you should expect to see _____.
  A. A weaker bull market in stocks
  B. A stronger than average bull market in stocks
  C. Nothing out of the ordinary
  D. A weak commodity bull market

7. When a recovery extends well beyond the normal 4 years without undergoing a recession but the growth rate slows down noticeably in the middle, _____.
  A. This is known as a double cycle.
  B. The financial markets do not experience the usual chronological sequence.
  C. The financial markets do experience the usual chronological sequence.
  D. A and C.

8. Knowing there is a chronological sequence of financial markets is very interesting, but how can technical analysis be used to identify these points?
A. By trial and error
B. Using long-term moving averages and other techniques for individual markets
C. Identifying the position of each market with several technical indicators and relating them to each other as a cross check
D. None of the above

9. Please fill in the blank:

When bonds and stocks are bullish and commodities are bearish, this is Stage _____ II _____.

10. Which industry groups have a tendency to do well in Stages IV and V?
A. Earnings driven
B. Liquidity driven
C. All groups
D. Groups sensitive to interest-rate movements

2

The Relationship Between the Financial Markets and the Business Cycle

Answers

1. D.

2. A.

3. B.

4. **B.** Each cycle has its own characteristics in that distortions develop in different sectors. For example, in 1970 it was housing, in 1973 it was in the commodity arena, in the mid-1980s it was in the S&Ls, and so forth.

5. **B.** Growth recessions still experience the financial market cycle.

6. B.

7. D.

8. **C.** B is correct as far as it goes, but C is a more complete answer because it uses the weight of the evidence approach.

9. **Stage II.**

10. A.

3
Dow Theory

Questions

Subjects to Be Covered

The concept
The tenets of the theory
Who developed Dow theory
How turning points are recognized
The limitations of the theory

1. Which of the following statements are correct?
    A. Dow theory is not concerned with the direction of a move, only its duration.
    B. Dow theory is not concerned with the duration of a move, only its direction.
    C. Dow theory is concerned with both the direction and duration of a move.
    D. None of the above.

2. Which of these statements is incorrect?
    A. Dow was concerned with forecasting stock prices.
    B. Dow developed and called the Dow theory after himself.
    C. Dow was concerned with forecasting business conditions through the use of stock prices.
    D. A and B.

3. What is the signal that triggers a primary bull trend?
   A. A series of rising intermediate peaks and troughs by either average
   B. A dividend yield in the DJIA in excess of 6 percent
   C. Both averages confirming a series of rising intermediate peaks and
      troughs
   D. A and B

4. Which of the following are basic tenets of Dow theory?
   A. The averages discount everything.
   B. The DJIA must yield less than 3 percent before a top can be
      signaled.
   C. Price action determines the trend.
   D. Lines form at market tops but only after the DJIA yields less than
      3 percent.
   E. The averages must confirm.
   F. Volume must expand on declines.
   G. A, B, E, and F.
   H. A, C, and E.

5. Who developed Dow's principles and organized them into something
   approaching the theory as we know it today?
   A. Dow
   B. Robert Rhea
   C. William Peter Hamilton
   D. Gartley

6. When compared to the buy-hold approach, Dow theory works just as
   well in secular bull markets as in multiyear trading ranges.
   A. True
   B. False

7. Looking at the following chart featuring intermediate rallies and
   reactions, what is happening at point A?
   A. A Dow theory buy signal
   B. A Dow theory sell signal
   C. A sell signal by the industrials that is unconfirmed by the
      transports
   D. A sell signal by the transports that is unconfirmed by the
      industrials

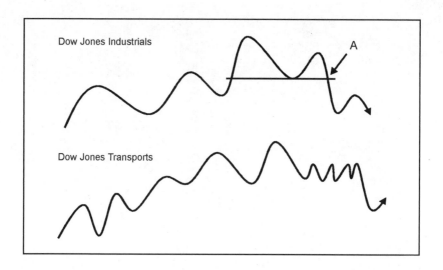

8. Which of these statements is correct?
   A. Dow theory is easy to interpret if you follow the rules exactly.
   B. Dow theory often leaves the analyst in doubt because it is sometimes difficult to identify intermediate price movements.
   C. Because Dow theory has beaten the buy-hold approach for most of the twentieth century, it will continue to do so in the twenty-first.
   D. None of the above.

9. Which of the following are not tenets of Dow theory?
   A. The averages discount everything.
   B. The averages must confirm.
   C. Volume is an integral part of the theory.
   D. Price action determines the trend.
   E. A, B, and C.
   F. A and B.

10. If Dow theory unequivocally signals a primary trend reversal, this

_____.

   A. Guarantees that the primary trend has reversed
   B. Is one piece of evidence, and a very important one, that the primary trend has reversed
   C. Is unlikely to result in a bear market because the theory is outdated
   D. Means that the size of the previous primary trend can be used as a basis for forecasting the duration and magnitude of the next primary trend
   E. B and D

3
Dow Theory

Answers

1. **B.**

2. **B.**

3. **C.**

4. **H.**

5. **C.**

6. **B.** Dow theory tends to give whipsaws in strong secular bull markets.

7. **C.** The industrials trigger a sell signal, but the transports continue to trace out a line formation. When the price breaks below the lower level of the line, a confirmation is given and a Dow theory bear market is confirmed.

8. **B.**

9. **C.** Volume is a background factor used to help interpret market turning points, not an integral part of the theory.

10. **B.** Dow theory offers just one piece of evidence that the trend has reversed. It certainly does not guarantee that a new primary trend is unfolding and definitely does not forecast the magnitude and duration of the next one. This is because there is no known method of accurately and consistently forecasting the magnitude and duration of a forthcoming price trend.

4
Typical Parameters for Intermediate Trends

Questions

Subjects to Be Covered

The relationship between intermediate and primary trends
The importance of intermediate trends
Differentiating between pro- and countertrends
Reasons for intermediate trends
The nature of intermediate trends

1. Why is it helpful to have an understanding of the character and duration of a typical intermediate trend?
   A. To help assess when the next short-term trend will begin
   B. To help assess when the next primary trend is likely to begin
   C. To improve success rates in trading
   D. B and C

2. Recognizing that there are numerous exceptions to this rule, in classic technical theory, how many primary intermediate price movements does a primary trend comprise?
   A. Seven
   B. Three
   C. Five
   D. None of the above

3. A bear market intermediate rally _____.
   A. Typically lasts for 2 weeks
   B. Is a counter cyclical trend

   C. Sometimes develops at the end of a bull market
   D. None of the above

4. Which of the following apply to an intermediate correction in a bull
   market?
   A. They can be extremely treacherous.
   B. They are usually easy to short and can therefore be extremely
      profitable.
   C. Last longer than an intermediate price movement.
   D. A and C.

5. Which of the following are legitimate causes for an intermediate
   correction in a bull market?
   A. Deteriorating political climate
   B. Falling interest rates
   C. Rising interest rates
   D. Reduced expectations for corporate profits
   E. Traders covering short positions
   F. A, B, and E
   G. A, C, and D

6. Based on Gartley's observation for the stock market between 1895 and
   1935, how many phases of liquidation is the norm for an intermediate
   correction in a bull market?
   A. One
   B. Two
   C. Three
   D. None of the above

7. A secondary correction must be an upward or downward price
   movement.
   A. True
   B. False

8. What is the difference between a primary intermediate price
   movement and a secondary reaction?
   A. A secondary reaction develops in a bull market and a primary
      intermediate price movement develops in a bear market.
   B. A primary intermediate price movement develops in a bull market
      and a secondary reaction develops in a bear market.
   C. A primary intermediate price movement develops in the direction
      of the main trend, a secondary reaction is a countercyclical price
      movement.
   D. None of the above.

9. Intermediate trends in security prices are determined by
   _____.
   A. The attitude of market participants to the emerging fundamentals
   B. The level of interest rates
   C. Corporate profits and other fundamentals
   D. None of the above

10. As a general tendency, which statement is correct?
   A. The larger the preceding intermediate rally, the larger the retracement.
   B. The smaller the preceding intermediate decline in a bear market, the smaller the bear market rally.
   C. The larger the intermediate rally in a bull market, the smaller the retracement move.
   D. None of the above.

4

Typical Parameters for Intermediate Trends

Answers

1. **D.** The correct identification of intermediate trends has a dual function. First, it functions as evidence that the prevailing primary trend is about to or has just reversed. Since intermediate price movements last for many weeks or even months, they provide useful trading opportunities.

2. **C.** Three is the established norm, but there are numerous exceptions to this rule. Trends should not be confused with cycles. Typically, there are two $1/2$ intermediate cycles in a primary bull market.

3. **B.** Typically, an intermediate bear market rally will last for a much shorter period than an intermediate rally in a bull market. The average for the former between 1932 and 1982 was 7 weeks and that of the latter was 24 weeks.

4. **A.** Contratrend moves are more liable to end up as whipsaws than pro-trend price movements.

5. **G.** At any one time there are four major influences on prices—psychological, technical, monetary, and economic. All represent legitimate reasons that justify a correction.

6. **B.** This is not true in every case, but the second wave of liquidation often heralds in the give-up phase when participants are so disgusted with the security in question that they are willing to throw in the towel at any cost.

7. B. Secondaries can also take the form of a sideways price movement.

8. C. Primary intermediate price movements tend to last much longer and experience greater magnitude than secondary corrections.

9. A. Although the level of interest rates and other fundamental factors are important, it is the *attitude* of market participants that is crucial. Often they will ignore factors that would previously have been the cause for an intermediate price movement and vice versa.

10. C. This is not always the case, but generally speaking, the stronger the rally, the weaker the retracement. Often toward the end of a secondary reaction in a bull market commentators reflect the view of many that prices are expected to correct much further; after all, they have only retraced a fraction of the previous advance. If this view is widespread, you can rest assured that the correction is probably over and that a new upleg is about to begin.

5
Price Patterns

Questions

Subjects to Be Covered

Transition phases in markets
Identification of price patterns
Ratio and arithmetic scaling
Significance of patterns
Measuring implications
Determining the validity of a breakout

1. To the market technician, the transitional phase has great significance because _____.
   A. It is easy to spot.
   B. It always takes the form of a V formation.
   C. It marks the turning point between a rising and a falling market and vice versa.
   D. A and B.

2. How are transition phases signaled in the markets?
   A. By monitoring stories in the media
   B. Adoption of the Dow theory
   C. Quiet market action
   D. By clearly definable price patterns or formations

3. The "line" formation developed from Dow theory is similar to
   _____.
   A. A triangle
   B. A flat head-and-shoulders top
   C. A rectangle
   D. None of the above

4. Please circle a head-and-shoulders top in the following chart.

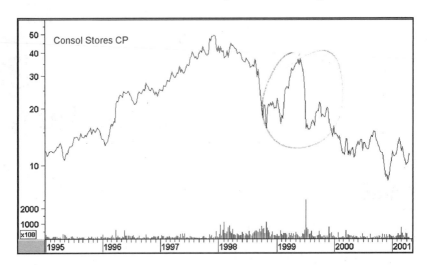

5. Please circle a double bottom in the following chart.

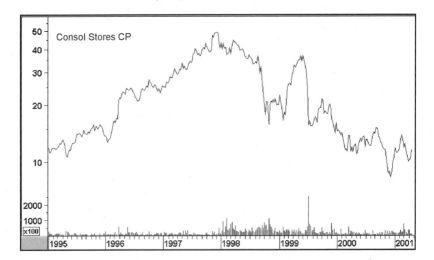

6. Please circle a failed reverse head and shoulders in this chart.

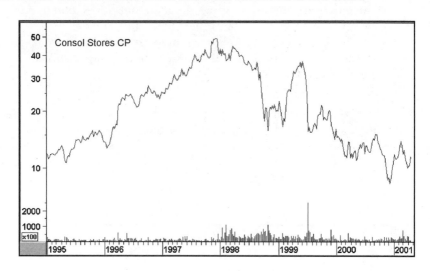

7. Why do you think the inverse head and shoulders in the previous chart failed?
- A. Because there was no appreciable increase in volume on the breakout.
- B. Because it was a countercyclical move.
- C. The pattern was too small.
- D. A and B.

8. Match the opposites. For example, A = D, B = F, and so on.
A. Distribution	A. Accumulation
B. Head-and-shoulders top	B. Descending right-angled triangle
C. Resistance	C. Inverse head and shoulders
D. Valid breakout	D. Contratrend move
E. Protrend move	E. Whipsaw
F. Ascending right-angled triangle	F. Support

A, C, F, E, D, B

9. With a ratio scale, each vertical inch represents a doubling in the price.
- A. True
- B. False

10. What advantage does the ratio scale have over an arithmetic scaling?
    A. All moves are measured proportionately and prices tend to move in proportion because they reflect human psychology.
    B. On long-term charts, price swings at lower levels are more visible.
    C. Measuring objectives from downside pattern completions are more accurate.
    D. All of the above.

11. During the formation of a price pattern, the direction of the breakout is not known. Therefore, you should assume _____.
    A. That the price will break in the direction of the prevailing trend
    B. That toppy-looking formations will break to the downside
    C. That formations that look like bases will break to the upside
    D. B and C

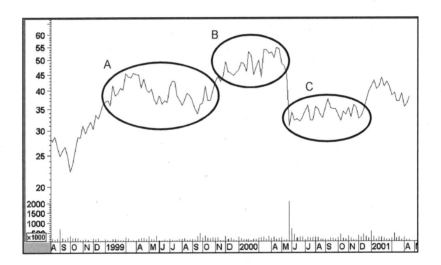

12. Which is the most important determinant of the significance of a price pattern?
    A. The strength of the rally of reaction preceding it
    B. Its size and depth
    C. A and B
    D. The amount of volume on the breakout

13. Name the patterns (or failed patterns) contained in the three ellipses:

A. _____

B. _____   *See chart*

C. _____

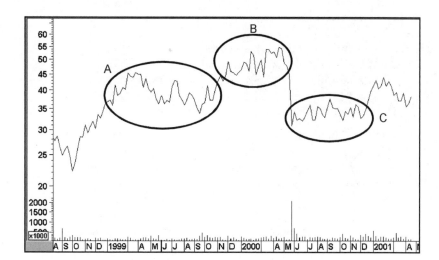

14. What is the difference in the measuring implication for a consolidation rectangle and a reversal rectangle? (Both are drawn on a ratio scale and have the same depth.)

A. The consolidation rectangle will have a greater price objective.

B. The reversal rectangle will have the larger price objective.

C. None.

D. The rectangle that took the longer to form will have the greater price objective.

15. Some of the factors that you should consider in determining the validity of a breakout are _____.

A. The volatility of a security

B. Whether the breakout holds for more than two sessions

C. The time frame of the chart (daily, intraday, weekly, and so on)

D. A and B

E. B and C

F. A, B, and C

16. The level of volume on an upside breakout is important.
- A. True
- B. False

17. The level of volume on a downside breakout is critical.
- A. True
- B. False

18. A head-and-shoulders top consists of _____.
- A. A final rally and two smaller rallies
- B. A final rally and at least three smaller rallies
- C. A final rally separated by two smaller rallies
- D. Two small rallies that precede a large rally

19. What are the distinguishing characteristics of an H&S top?
- A. Heavy volume on the right shoulder and head
- B. Light volume on the right shoulder and heavy volume on the downside breakout
- C. Heavy volume on the left shoulder and/or head, and light volume on the right shoulder
- D. Heavy volume on the left shoulder and heavy volume on the breakout

20. What are the distinguishing characteristics of an H&S bottom?
- A. A final decline separated by two smaller declines
- B. A noticeable expansion of volume during the formation of the right shoulder
- C. A noticeable expansion of volume during the breakout
- D. A and C

21. The volume level during the formation of the second top and second bottom in a double top and double bottom formation should be

_____.
- A. More volume for the second top and less volume for the second bottom
- B. Less volume for the second top and more volume for the second bottom
- C. Less volume in both instances than the initial top or bottom
- D. None of the above

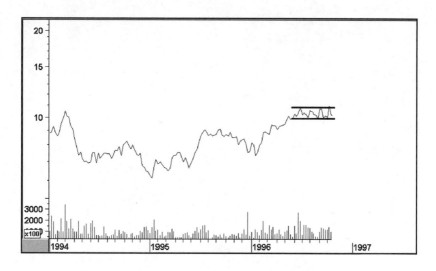

22. Triangles are generally more reliable than H&S tops.
    A. True
    B. False

23. Which direction is the breakout likely to come?
    A. Up
    B. Down

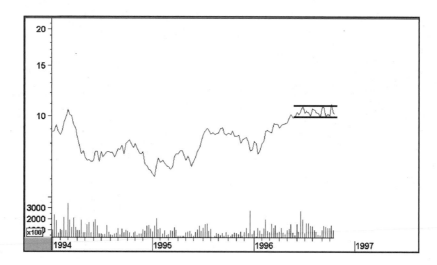

5
Price Patterns

Answers

1. **C.** These transitional periods typically show up on the charts as price formations or price patterns.

2. **D.** This is not always so, but it is usually the case.

3. **C.**

4. **The chart provides the answer.**

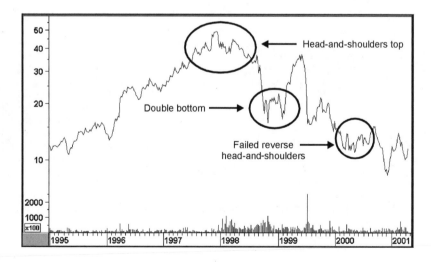

35

5. **The chart provides the answer.**

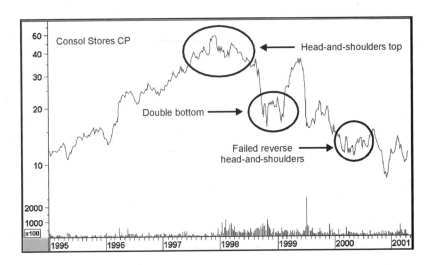

6. **The chart provides the answer.**

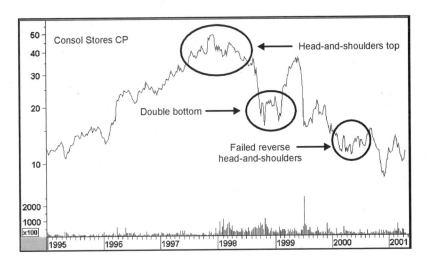

7. D.

8. A = A; **B** = C; **C** = F; **D** = E; **E** = D; **F** = B.

9. B. With a ratio scale, each vertical distance represents the same
proportionate move. It would depend on the scaling and how much

an inch represented. It could be anything, a doubling, a 10-percent move, a 25-percent move, and so on.

10. D.

11. A. It should always be assumed that the prevailing trend is intact until the weight of the evidence proves otherwise.

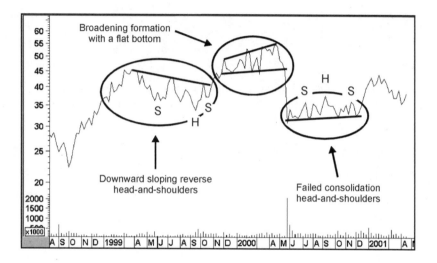

12. B. The longer a pattern takes to form, the greater the battle between buyers and sellers, and therefore the more significant the outcome.

13. See chart.

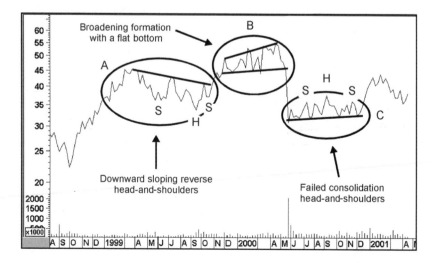

14. **C.** This is because the measuring objective comes from the depth, not the size of the pattern. Since both have the same depth, their measuring objectives will be identical.

15. **D.** The timeframe has no influence on the validity of a breakout, only its significance. A breakout on a daily chart is not as important as one on a monthly chart.

16. **A.**

17. **B.**

18. **C.**

19. **C.** The level of volume on a downside breakout is not important, but relatively light volume on the formation of the right shoulder is.

20. **D.**

21. **C.**

22. **B.** H&S are usually more reliable than triangles.

23. **A.** This is because it is always assumed that the prevailing trend is in force until proven otherwise. The answer is on the chart.

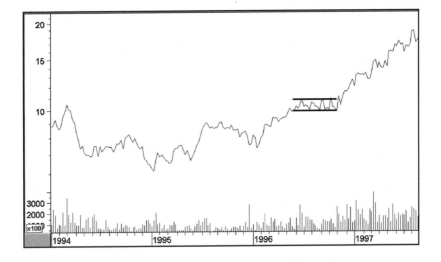

6

Smaller Price Patterns

Questions

Subjects to Be Covered

Differentiation between patterns
Pattern recognition
Types of gaps and their significance

1. How long does a typical flag take to form on a daily chart?
   A. 1 week
   B. 10 weeks
   C. 3 weeks
   D. 3 months

2. A pennant is formed with _____.
   A. Two converging trendlines
   B. Two diverging trendlines
   C. Two parallel lines
   D. Two parallel lines that slope down in a downtrend and up in an uptrend

3. None of the patterns shown in this chart are perfect. Based on the description in Chapter 6, "Smaller Price Patterns," which does pattern B most closely resemble?
   A. A pennant
   B. A flag
   C. A wedge
   D. None described

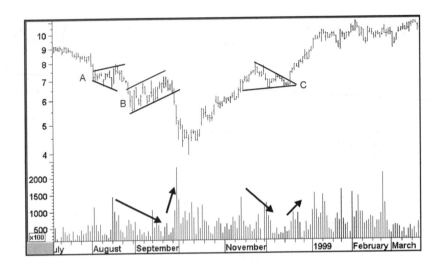

4. None of the patterns shown in the above chart are perfect. Based on
   the description in Chapter 6, which does pattern A most closely
   resemble?
   A. A pennant
   B. A flag
   C. A wedge
   D. None described

5. None of the patterns shown in the above chart are perfect. Based on
   the description in Chapter 6, which does pattern C most closely
   resemble?
   A. A pennant
   B. A flag
   C. A wedge
   D. None described

6. If a wedge develops in a bear market, what should you expect to see
   on the breakout in order to see a sharp price move?
   A. A noticeable expansion of volume and a decisive price break
   B. No expansion of volume and an indecisive break
   C. No noticeable pickup in volume but a decisive price break
   D. None of the above

7. What pattern has the following characteristics?
The price action is bounded by two rising converging lines. The pattern develops over a 3-week period on shrinking volume.
A. A bearish flag
B. A bullish wedge
C. A bearish pennant
D. None of the above

8. The volume action of a rounded top and a saucer bottom are vastly different.
A. True
B. False

9. Which of the following statements are correct?
 i. Gaps on intraday charts are always filled.
 ii. Gaps on all charts are usually filled.
 iii. Gaps are more common on weekly than daily charts.
 iv. Gaps are more common on intraday than daily charts.
A. i and ii
B. ii and iv
C. i and iv
D. i and iii

10. Please match the following. For example, A = C, B = A, and so on.
A. Breakaway gaps _____   A. Develop at the end of a trend
B. Area gaps _____   B. Develop during a trend
C. Exhaustion gaps _____   C. Develop during a trading range
D. Continuation gaps _____   D. Develop as a price is breaking out from a trading range

11. Please fill in the blanks:
A gap is an (A) em_____ point on a chart. The upper and lower points of a gap often become future (B) s_____ and (C) r_____ points.

12. Gaps are most common on _____.
A. Daily charts
B. Weekly charts
C. Intraday charts
D. They are equally common on all charts

6

Smaller Price Patterns

Answers

1. **C.** This is because it is a period of controlled profit or loss taking. Anything longer than 3 to 4 weeks is usually indicative of something else.

2. **A.** One line slopes up, and the other slopes down.

3. **B.** Ideally, a flag should be formed when the trend of volume is noticeably declining and shrinks to almost nothing, thereby indicating a fine balance between buyers and sellers. That's not true in this case, though volume certainly expands on the downside break.

4. **D.** These trendlines are diverging and do not correspond with any of the patterns described in Chapter 6. If anything, this is a small broadening formation.

5. **A.** Normally, a pennant would touch the lower trendline one more time and volume should shrink much more toward the apex. Also, the lower line would normally have a sharper angle of ascent than the one shown here.

6. **A.** An expansion of volume on a downside break is not mandatory, but if it does take place, it emphasizes the strength of the violation because it indicates selling pressure as opposed to a lack of buyers.

7. **D.** The description is of a bearish wedge, not a bullish wedge, where the two converging lines are declining.

8. **B.** The volume patterns are more or less identical. It is the price action that is totally different.

9. **B.** Gaps are usually, but not always filled. Since opening and classic gaps both appear on intraday charts and only classic gaps appear on daily charts, intraday charts experience more gaps.

10. **A** = D; **B** = C; **C** = A; **D** = B.

11. **A.** emotional; **B.** support; **C.** resistance.

12. **C.**

7

One- and Two-Bar Patterns

Questions

Subjects to Be Covered

Preconditions for one and two bar patterns
Differentiating between the various patterns
How they should be interpreted

1. To qualify, an outside bar must contain *all* the following elements:
   i. Should be preceded by a strong price trend
   ii. Should totally encompass the previous bar's trading range
   iii. Should gap up or down on the previous bar
   A. True
   B. False

2. Which of the following is not true?
   A. One- and two-bar patterns have only short-term significance.
   B. One- and two-bar patterns must be preceded by a strong price trend.
   C. When all of the characteristics are present, one- and two-bar patterns can always be relied upon to signal strong trend reversals.
   D. One- and two-bar patterns should be interpreted in terms of shades of gray rather than black or white.

3. Is the following chart correctly labeled?
   A. Yes
   B. No

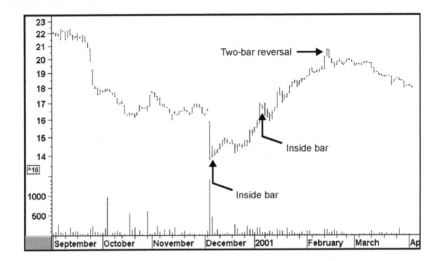

4. What is the difference between a one-bar island reversal and an exhaustion bar?
   A. The one-bar island reversal has a wider trading range.
   B. The exhaustion bar has a gap to the right of the bar.
   C. The one-bar island reversal only develops at tops.
   D. The one-bar island reversal leaves a gap on both sides; the exhaustion bar leaves a gap to the left.

5. What is the correct name for the two bars in the rectangle?
   A. An outside bar
   B. An inside bar
   C. A key-bar reversal
   D. A two-bar reversal

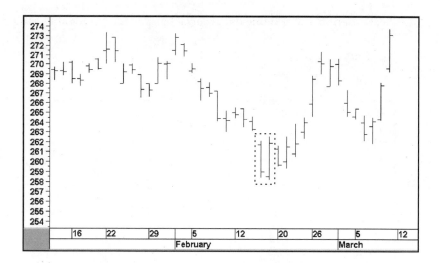

6. Other things being equal, which pattern is likely to be followed by the largest price move?
   A. A key reversal on a 10-minute bar chart
   B. A two-bar reversal with all the correct characteristics on a 5-minute bar chart
   C. An inside bar on a daily chart
   D. An exhaustion bar with all the correct characteristics on a 30-minute bar chart

7. Name the pattern with the following characteristics:

   The first bar is long following a sustained up- or down-trend.

   The second bar is much shorter. Its trading range is totally within that of the first bar.

   Volume is lower on the second bar.

   A. Outside bar
   B. Inside bar
   C. Love reversal
   D. Key reversal

8. Please identify the two one-day reversal bar patterns in the following chart:
   A.
   B. _____

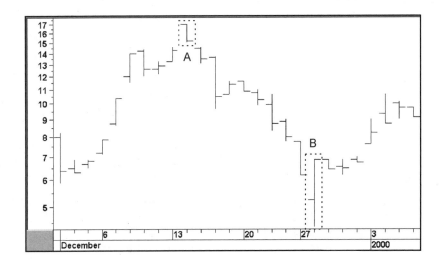

9. Two-bar reversals differ from inside bars in which of the following ways?
   A. There is no essential difference.
   B. The inside bar is smaller than the bar in a two-bar reversal.
   C. The two bars in two-bar reversals only form at tops; insde bars form at tops and bottoms.
   D. None of the above.

10. Since one- and two-bar price patterns are only of short-term significance, they never form at bull market peaks or bear market lows.
    A. True
    B. False

7
One- and Two-Bar Patterns

Answers

1. **B.** Gapping up or down on a precious bar is not a requirement.

2. **C.** This is a false statement because technical analysis deals in probabilities, *never* certainties.

3. **A.** The second bar is an outside bar, but the question asked for the name of the pattern describing *two* bars.

4. **D.**

5. **D.**

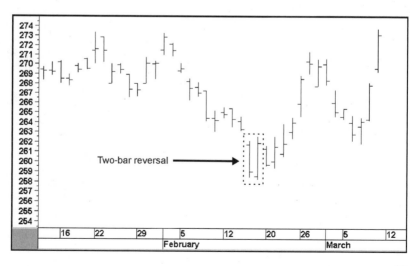

6. **C.** This is the correct answer because a one- or two-bar pattern derives its significance from the amount of time taken to complete it.

7. **B.**

8. **A.** This is a one-day island reversal. **B** is a key reversal bar.

9. **B.**

10. **B.** They may have short-term significance, but there is no reason why they cannot appear at major peaks and troughs. In fact, they often do.

8
Trendlines

Questions

Subjects to Be Covered

Trendlines
Types of trendline break
Determining the significance of trendlines
Ratio and arithmetic scaling
Extended trendlines

1. How many times must a line be touched to qualify as a trendline?
   A. Once
   B. Three times
   C. Twice
   D. None of the above

2. Which trendline has the greatest significance?
   A. A 10-minute trendline
   B. A 5-year trendline
   C. A 2-year trendline
   D. A 10-year trendline

3. What are the two types of trendline breaks?
   A. c_____
   B. r_____

4. Construct a trendline on the following chart that best reflects the underlying downtrend.

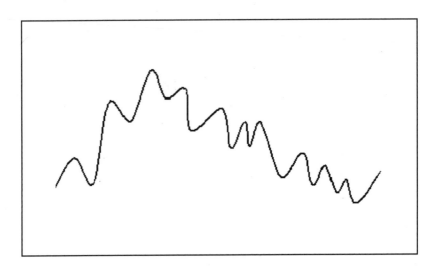

5. If a trendline is violated and a reversal price pattern is completed at roughly the same time, what can you conclude?
   A. That prices will consolidate around the prevailing trend
   B. That the prevailing trend will extend
   C. That the trend will reverse
   D. That the trend will initially reverse and then continue in its previous direction

6. Which is the most significant trendline on the following chart based on the principles outlined in the text? Tip: The correct line is not necessarily the one followed by the biggest move.
   A. _____
   B. _____
   C. _____

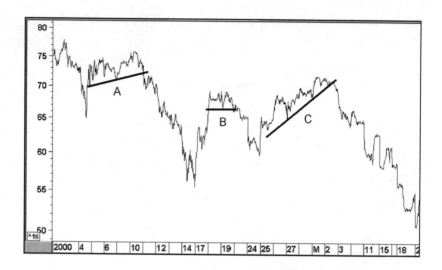

7. Which is the correct statement?
   A. Uptrendlines are violated quicker on a ratio scale and downtrendlines are violated quicker on an arithmetic scale.
   B. Downtrendlines are violated quicker on a ratio scale and up-trendlines are violated quicker on an arithmetic scale.
   C. Uptrendlines are violated quicker on a ratio scale and on an arithmetic scale.
   D. Downtrendlines are violated quicker on a ratio scale and on an arithmetic scale.

8. In the following chart, is the measuring objective drawn correctly?
   A. Yes
   B. No

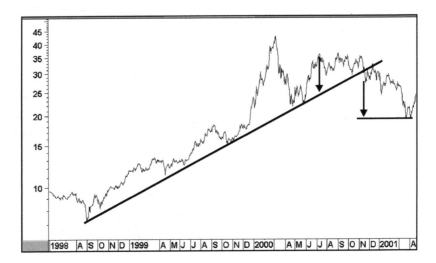

9. Fill in the missing words:

   When two down-trendlines can be drawn in parallel fashion, this is known as a trend (A) c_____. In a rising market, the upper line is known as a (B) r _____line.

10. What is the characteristic being represented in the following chart?

   e_____

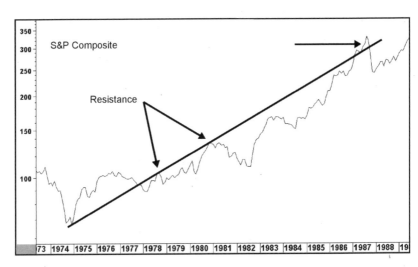

11. What is the principle being reflected in the following chart?

c_____ f_____ principle

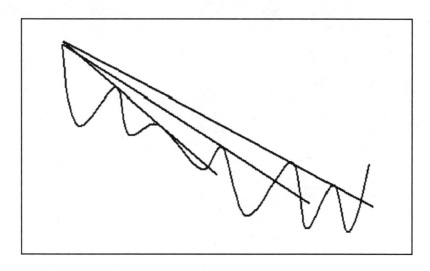

12. Once a trendline has been violated, _____.
   A. You can forget about it.
   B. Draw another line.
   C. Extend it to look for future support/resistance levels.
   D. None of the above.

13. A trendline that touches only one point is _____.
   A. A good trendline
   B. A poor trendline
   C. Likely to be penetrated soon
   D. Not a trendline

14. Trendlines obtain their significance from three things. What are they?
   A. The _____.
   B. The number of times it has been _____ or approached.
   C. The A_____ of ascent or descent.

15. Please fill in the blanks:

A trendline is a dynamic area of (A) s_____ and (B) r_____.

8
Trendlines

Answers

1. **C.** A trendline that has only been touched once is not a real trendline because it could be drawn at virtually any angle and would not reflect the underlying trend.

2. **D.** The longer the line, the greater its significance.

3. **A.** reversal; **B.** continuation.

4. **See chart.** This line has been touched more times than a line that would have been constructed from the high to the whipsaw high.

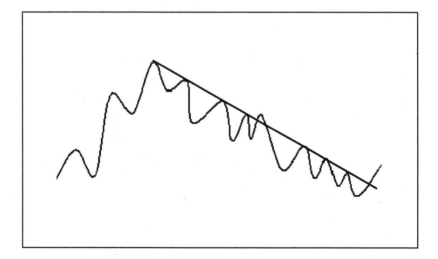

5. **C.** The completion of the price pattern indicates that a reversal is likely.

6. **C.** Because it is longer, has been touched or approached on several occasions, and is not too steep.

7. **A.**

8. **B.** The measuring objective is calculated by taking the maximum distance between the price and the trendline. In this case the bull market peak in early 2000 would have been the place to take the measurement, not the July top.

9. **A.** channel; **B.** return.

10. **Exhaustion.**

11. **The corrective fan principle** (score even if you missed the word "corrective").

12. **C.** An extended line can often be of great significance. If the price ever returns to it, the trendline's former role is then reversed. What was support now becomes resistance and vice versa.

13. **D.** A trendline that touches one point is a line drawn in space and is unlikely to reflect the underlying trend.

14. **A.** The length of the line; **B.** The number of times it has been touched or approached; **C.** The angle of ascent or descent.

15. **A.** support; **B.** resistance.

9

Moving Averages

Questions

Subjects to Be Covered

Types of moving averages
Centering averages
Determining the significance of a crossover
Establishing the validity of a crossover
The importance of time spans
Advancing averages
Comparing more than one average
Interpreting Bollinger bands

1. Please fill in the blanks:

   A weighted moving average (A) f_____ loads the data.
   A (B) s_____ moving average treats all the data equally.
   An (C) e_____ moving average front loads the data.

2. Which of the following statements is true?
   A. A centered moving average is more accurate in reflecting trend changes, but less timely in triggering signals.
   B. A noncentered moving average triggers buy and sell signals when it experiences a price crossover.
   C. The shorter the time span, the greater the sensitivity of a moving average.
   D. All of the above.
   E. B and C.

3. Other things being equal, which is likely to result in the most reliable signal?
   A. A crossover that takes place when the MA is rising sharply
   B. A crossover that develops when the average is relatively flat
   C. A crossover that develops when the MA is falling sharply
   D. A and C

4. Which statement is incorrect?
   A. The shorter the time span, the more significant the signal.
   B. The longer the time span, the more significant the signal.
   C. Changes in direction of a moving average are more significant than crossovers.
   D. B and C.

5. The 3 percent crossover rule is suited to an MA with a time span of
   _____.
   A. 10 days
   B. 10 weeks
   C. 40 weeks
   D. 120 hours

6. If you were going to plot two averages on a chart, which combination would make sense?
   A. 10 and 11 days
   B. 3- and 65-week EMA
   C. 10 and 25 days
   D. 30 and 31 hours

7. An advanced moving average often avoids whipsaws, but what is the tradeoff?
   A. There is none.
   B. Some signals are less timely.
   C. There are too many signals.
   D. B and C.

8. Trendlines can make moving average analysis more effective.
   A. True
   B. False

9. When three moving averages of a relatively different time span converge, what does this indicate?
   A. The balance between buyers and sellers is evenly matched.
   B. The price is set up ready for a relatively large move in either direction.

    C. They will soon cross each other.
    D. A and B.
    E. A and C.

10. Which of the averages in the following chart is likely to be weighted?
    A. The dashed line
    B. The solid line

11. Bollinger bands _____.
    A. Widen as prices become less volatile
    B. Narrow after a big move
    C. Widen as prices become more volatile
    D. None of the above

12. A high-standard deviation factor for Bollinger bands
    _____.
    A. Makes them diverge from the price unduly so they are of little
       practical use
    B. Offers more signals
    C. Does not have any effect on their appearance because the choice
       of moving average time span is more important
    D. A and C

Moving Averages

Answers

1. **A.** front; **B.** simple; **C.** exponential.

2. **D.**

3. **B.**

4. **A.**

5. **C.**

6. **C.** All other combinations are either too close or spaced too widely to be of any use.

7. **B.**

8. **A.**

9. **D.**

10. **B.** The solid line turns faster because it is front loaded. Both averages in the chart have a time span of 50 days.

11. **C.**

12. **A.**

10
Momentum I
Basic Principles

Questions

Subjects to Be Covered

Terminology
Broad categories of interpretation
Differentiating between price and breadth momentum
Limitations of oscillators
Megaoverboughts and oversolds
Extreme swings
Price discrepancy divergences
Complex divergences
Methods of ROC calculation

1. Match up the following:

A. Rate of change	_____	A. Smooth and deliberate indicator confined between 0 and 100
B. RSI	_____	B. A form of trend deviation indicator
C. Overbought/oversold	_____	C. Sign of a potential top
D. Stochastics	_____	D. Jagged indicator with no upside finite boundaries
E. MACD	_____	E. Not to be confused with comparative relative strength
F. Positive divergence	_____	F. Sign of a potential bottom
G. Negative divergence	_____	G. Measures extreme moves
H. Momentum is a	_____	H. Generic term

2. If you spot a negative divergence, you should _____.
    A. Sell immediately
    B. Watch to see if the divergence is confirmed by a trend break in the price and then sell
    C. Buy more
    D. None of the above

3. What are the two broad categories of momentum interpretation?
    A. c_____
    B. t_____
    C. r_____

4. The interpretation of price and breadth momentum _____.
    A. Is more or less identical
    B. Is totally different
    C. Depends on the time span
    D. None of the above

5. When a security's price is in a linear uptrend, _____.
    A. It indicates that the momentum indicator will operate more accurately than normal.
    B. It will always experience numerous divergences.
    C. A and B.
    D. Momentum indicators will normally fail to operate, which is why we need to await some kind of confirmation from the price.

6. Which conditions does a mega overbought require?
    A. To be preceded by a primary bull market and reach a multiyear overbought reading
    B. To be preceded by a mega oversold condition and reach a multiyear overbought condition
    C. To reach a multiyear overbought condition and diverge positively with the price
    D. To be preceded by a primary bear market and reach a multiyear overbought condition

7. Name the momentum phenomenon at point A in the following chart.
    A. Mega oversold
    B. Negative price discrepancy divergence
    C. Bullish extreme swing
    D. Bearish extreme swing

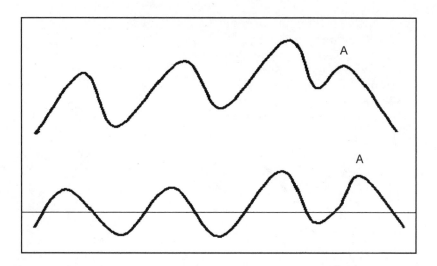

8. Name the momentum phenomenon that begins at point A in the following chart.
   A. Mega oversold
   B. Negative price discrepancy divergence
   C. Bullish extreme swing
   D. Bearish extreme swing

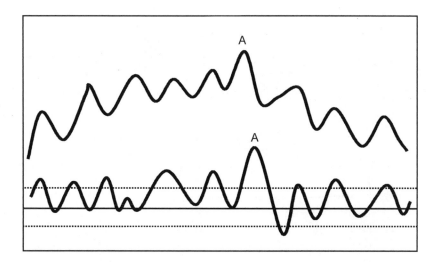

9. Name the momentum phenomenon at point A in the following chart.
   A. Mega oversold
   B. Price discrepancy divergence
   C. None of these answers
   D. Bearish extreme swing

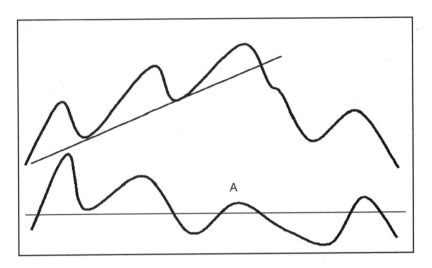

10. Fill in the blank:

When an oscillator is constructed from price, it is known as price momentum. When constructed from a basket of items, it is known as b_____ momentum.

11. Divergences signal that a trend has reversed.
   A. True
   B. False

12. In order to spot a complex divergence, _____.
   A. It's first necessary to plot two different indicators using identical time spans.
   B. Two indicators where the time spans are very similar in order to make sure that they confirm each other.
   C. Three indicators plotted with widely differing time spans.
   D. Two indicators plotted with widely differing time spans overlaid on each other.

13. If the price and momentum simultaneously violate trendlines, the resulting price move is likely to be weaker.
  A. True
  B. False

14. If prices are not experiencing normal cyclic rhythm, then
  _____.
  A. The interpretation of oscillators is made much easier.
  B. The price is experiencing a linear uptrend.
  C. Momentum interpretation may not work so well.
  D. The price is in a linear downtrend.
  E. None of the above are correct statements.

15. The ROC, over very long periods, is best calculated using the
  _____.
  A. Subtraction method
  B. Division method

16. Which statement best describes a mega oversold?
  A. An extreme overbought following a bull market that is then followed by an extreme oversold
  B. A multiyear overbought reading that follows a primary bear market
  C. A multiyear oversold reading that follows a primary bull market
  D. A multiyear overbought reading accompanied by expanding volume that follows a primary bear market

17. Which statement is incorrect?
  A. An ROC lends itself to trendline construction but should not be used with MAs.
  B. An ROC lends itself to price pattern construction.
  C. An MA lends itself to trendline construction, price pattern construction, and divergences.
  D. None of these statements are incorrect.

18. Zero crossovers by oscillators should never be used because they throw up too many whipsaws.
  A. True
  B. False

10
Momentum I
Basic Principles

Answers

1. **A** = D; **B** = E; **C** = G; **D** = A; **E** = B; **F** = F; **G** = C; **H** = H.

2. **B.** It is important to await a price confirmation because you do not know if another divergence will develop.

3. **A.** characteristics; **B.** trend reversals.

4. **A.**

5. **D.**

6. **D.**

7. **B.**

8. **D.**

9. **C.** This is an example of the oscillator barely rising above the equilibrium level following a negative divergence. Such action, when confirmed by the price, is usually followed by an above average decline.

10. **Breadth.**

11. **B.** Only price can signal a trend reversal. Divergences merely tell us whether the underlying momentum is getting weaker or stronger. False is therefore the correct answer.

12. **D.**

13. B. When a simultaneous break develops, the signal is usually much stronger.

14. C. The use of oscillators assumes that the price is undergoing a normal cyclic rhythm. Oscillators do not work well in linear up- or downtrends or any other type of trend where normal cyclic activity is not being experienced.

15. B. It does not matter much over the very short term which method is adopted. However, over long periods of time when prices advance or decline significantly, the subtraction method will distort the indicator's readings.

16. C.

17. A. This statement is incorrect because ROCs can be used with MAs.

18. B. Most of the time zero crossovers will throw up too many whipsaws to be of any practical use. However, there are exceptions, especially when longer-term timeframes are used. Reference should always be made to a long-term historical record to ensure that this approach works for the security and timeframe selected.

11
Individual Momentum Indicators I

Questions

Subjects to Be Covered

RSI versus the ROC
Overbought/oversold lines for the RSI
Interpreting the RSI
The CMO versus the RSI and RMI
Calculating the trend deviation indicator
Interpreting the MACD
The concept behind the construction of the stochastic
Differentiating between percent K and percent D

1. Name two useful advantages that the RSI has over the ROC.
   i. It is smoother.
   ii. It is confined between 0 and 100.
   iii. It is easier to compare the momentum of different securities.
   iv. It always throws up actionable divergences.
   v. It is useful for zero crossovers.
   A. i and v
   B. i, ii, and iii
   C. ii, iii, iv, and v
   D. i, iv, and v

2. What are the default overbought/oversold bands for a 14-day RSI?
   A. 80 to 20
   B. 60 to 40
   C. 20 to 30
   D. None of the above

3. The RSI is more volatile the shorter the time span.
   A. True
   B. False

4. Which letter in the following chart corresponds with a bearish failure swing?
   A.
   B.
   C.
   D.
   E. None of the above

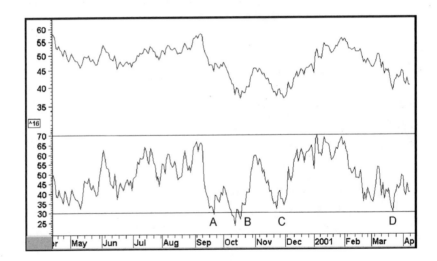

5. Name one advantage that the CMO has over the RSI.
   A. It reaches overbought/oversold extremes more often.
   B. It is extremely smooth and deliberate in its trajectory.
   C. It never gives false signals.
   D. A and B.

6. In the following chart, which of the two RSIs is more likely to be plotted from a 6-day time span?
   A. The one in the center panel
   B. The one in the lower panel

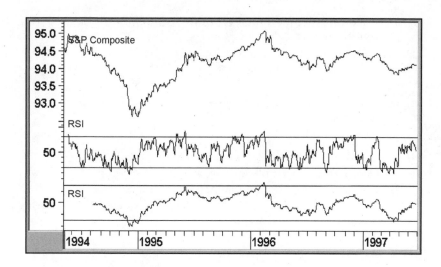

7. Please match the following answers:
   A. RSI   _____   A. Relative strength indicator
   B. Bearish failure swing   _____   B. Relatively smooth and
                                                         deliberate trading band
   C. Chaunde Momentum _____   C. Relative Momentum Index
      Oscillator
   D. 9-day RSI   _____   D. 70/30 overbought/oversold
                                                         defaults
   E. 45-week RSI   _____   E. Associated with a reversal from
                                                         an uptrend to a downtrend
   F. RSI 14-day time span _____   F. Volatile trading action
   G. RMI   _____   G. CMO

8. The RSI can be interpreted by using reversals in peak-trough
   progressions.
   A. False, because it is too volatile
   B. True
   C. Yes, but only on monthly charts because intraday, daily, and weekly
      are too volatile
   D. Only after a failure swing

 9. The following momentum interpretive techniques can be used with
 the RSI.
   A. Trendline and price pattern analysis
   B. Moving average analysis
   C. Failure swings
   D. Overbought/oversold analysis
   E. A, B, and C
   F. A, B, C, and D

10. A trend deviation indicator is calculated by _____.
   A. Comparing two simple moving averages
   B. Comparing two exponential moving averages
   C. Expressing the closing price as a deviation of a weighted moving
      average
   D. A and B
   E. A, B, and C

11. There is no difference between the MACD and a trend deviation
 indicator.
   A. True
   B. False

12. According to the text, an MACD is best interpreted using

 _____.
   A. The signal line
   B. Trendline violations and overbought/oversold crossovers
   C. Complex divergences
   D. Megareverse divergences

13. The calculation of the stochastics indicator assumes the price closes

 _____.
   A. Close to the middle of its trading range in the middle of a trend
   B. Close to the low at the start of an uptrend and close to the high at
      the end
   C. Close to the low at the end of an uptrend and close to its high at
      the end of a downtrend
   D. Close to the open at the end of a downtrend

14. In stochastic interpretation, a right-hand crossover is considered to be a more powerful signal than a left-hand one.
  A. True
  B. False

15. Which is the faster of the two stochastic indicators?
  A. Percent D
  B. Percent K

11

Individual Momentum Indicators I

Answers

1. **B.**

2. **D.** 70/30 is the correct default.

3. **A.**

4. **E.** B happens to be a bullish failure swing, but the question asked for a bearish one.

5. **A.** It reaches overbought and oversold extremes more often and therefore lends itself better to overbought/oversold analysis.

6. **A.** This is because it is more volatile. The shorter the time span, the more volatile the indicator.

7. **A** = A; **B** = E; **C** = G; **D** = F; **E** = B; **F** = D; **G** = C.

8. **B.**

9. **F.**

10. **E.**

11. **A.** An MACD is a form of trend deviation indicator.

12. **B.** Signal line crossovers are considered by many to offer good signals, especially if the chosen parameters result in a smooth indicator, but the text indicates that there are numerous whipsaws that are triggered from this approach using the default values on daily charts. There is no such concept as a megareverse divergence.

13. C.

14. A.

15. B. Remember K = Kwick and D= Dawdle.

12

Individual Momentum Indicators II

Questions

Subjects to Be Covered

RSI versus the ROC
Terminology for the directional movement system
Suitable timeframes and interpretation of the ADX
DI interpretation
Calculation of the KST
Interpretation of the KST
Parameter requirements for the parabolic

1. Plus DI stands for _____.
   A. Positive distance indicator
   B. Positive directional movement
   C. Directional indicator
   D. None of the above

2. If you know the probabilities favor that directional movement is
   increasing, it's okay _____.
   A. To buy
   B. To sell
   C. To look at other indicators to see which direction the price trend
      is likely to move in and then take action
   D. Buy calls

3. The following chart features two ADXs. Which one is calculated from the shorter time span?
   A. The one in the center panel
   B. The one in the lower panel

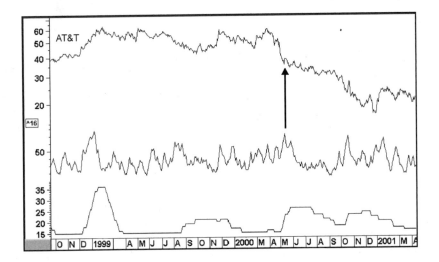

4. At point A in the following chart, what factors suggest the rising price trend will continue?
   A. The breakout from the inverse head and shoulders in the price
   B. The breakout by the ADX
   C. The plus DI remains above the minus DI
   D. A and B
   E. B and C
   F. A, B, and C

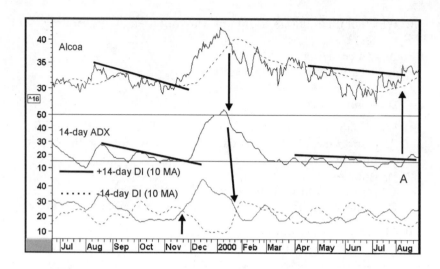

5. A 14-day ADX reading that peaks from above 40 tells you
_____.
A. The price is about to rally.
B. Directional movement has now peaked and we should look for a significant change in trend.
C. Directional movement has peaked but we do not know the significance.
D. None of the above.

6. The plus DI crosses below the minus DI and the price completes a head-and-shoulders top. We should _____.
A. Do nothing until we can observe a peaking in the ADX.
B. Sell.
C. Wait for the smoothed DIs to cross.
D. A and C.

7. How many ROC timeframes are used in the KST formula?
A. One
B. Six
C. Four
D. Three

8. Which of the following techniques are not used in interpreting the KST?

    A. MA crossovers

    B. Trendline analysis

    C. Divergences

    D. Complex crossovers

9. Which signal is likely to be followed by the largest trend reversal?

    A. A short-term KST buy signal and trendline violation by the intermediate KST

    B. A long-term KST buy signal from above zero

    C. A price-confirmed long-term KST buy signal from below zero

    D. A short-term KST buy, an intermediate buy, and a trendline break

10. The KST tends to work because _____.

    A. It is constructed from four different time spans that reflect different cycles.

    B. It is weighted to give more dominance to the longer cycles.

    C. It has been rigorously tested.

    D. A and B.

    E. A, B, and C.

11. What are the parameters for the parabolic?

    A. The time span of the average and the acceleration factor

    B. The acceleration factor and the maximum immune quotient

    C. The acceleration factor and the maximum acceleration factor

    D. None of the above

12. The parabolic can be used as a stop-and-reversal system.

    A. True

    B. False

12
Individual Momentum Indicators II

Answers

1. **B.**

2. **C.** Since you do not know which the direction the price is likely to trend, it's important to check out other indicators such as plus DI and minus DI.

3. **A.** The center panel contains a 6-day ADX, and the lower one contains a 30-day ADX.

4. **F.**

5. **C.** Since each security has different levels of volatility, we do not know the significance of the 40 level unless we can look at past history. All we know is that directional movement has peaked, but we do not know the significance.

6. **B.** The DI crossover is a momentum sell signal and the head and shoulders is the price trend confirmation. Therefore, based on this information the correct thing to do is sell.

7. **C.**

8. **D.** There is no such thing as a complex crossover; there are only complex divergences.

9. **C.** The long-term KST is the dominant one and therefore provides the most significant signals.

10. D. The KST may have been tested, but it would not work not because it had been tested, but because it was carefully designed. The testing would have been a by-product.

11. C.

12. A. It is not recommended though because it will trigger contratrend signals when used in this way.

13
Candlesticks

Questions

Subjects to Be Covered

Candle construction
Differentiating between and recognizing the various patterns
Advantages of candle volume

1. Candle charts consist of _____.
   A. Opening prices
   B. Closing prices
   C. A real body
   D. A wick
   E. A and C
   F. C and D

2. If I only have price data for the high, low, and close, which patterns will not show up correctly in candle charts?
   A. Engulfing patterns
   B. Dojis
   C. Meeting lines
   D. None of the above

3. Please fill in the gaps:

   In candle charting, the greatest emphasis is placed on the (A) o_____ and (B) c_____ price.

4. What is the highlighted candle pattern in this chart?
   A. A bearish engulfing
   B. A piercing line
   C. A dark cloud cover
   D. None of the above

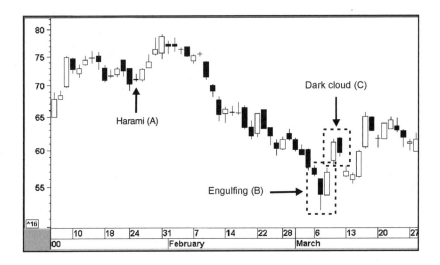

5. A hammer appears at a bottom and a hanging man at a top.
   A. True
   B. False

6. Please fill in the gaps:

A candle where the real body is small and develops at the high end of the session's trading range is called a(n) u_____.

7. Are the patterns in the following chart labeled correctly?
   A. _____
   B. _____
   C. _____

8. Which, if any, of the following are reversal patterns?
   A. Rising three methods
   B. Falling three methods
   C. Upside gap (tasuki)
   D. Shooting star

9. Candle volume charts are helpful because _____.
   A. It's easy to spot candles where volume is heavy or light and then to relate these characteristics to the price action.
   B. It's possible to display more candles in the same space.
   C. More reversal candle patterns are displayed.
   D. A and C.

10. Which of the following is not a true statement?
   A. Candles can be plotted for any timeframe.
   B. Candle charting cannot be used with western charting techniques.
   C. Candle charting is enhanced when used with western charting techniques.
   D. All of the above.

11. Following a rally, two white candles have identical closing prices. Is this a tweezer top?
   A. Yes.
   B. No.
   C. It will depend on whether the closes represented the highs for the session.

12. Which of the following correctly describes a counterattack line?
   A. Two candles with long real bodies following an advance of differing colors with identical closing price
   B. Two candles with long real bodies following a decline where the first is black, the second is white, and their opening prices are identical
   C. Two candles with long real bodies following a decline where the first is white, the second is black, and their opening prices are identical
   D. Two candles with long real bodies following a decline where the first is black, the second is white, and their closing prices are identical

13. Which answer best describes a bullish belt hold?

    A. A long white line

    B. A small real body the develops after a decline

    C. A long white line that develops after a decline

    D. An unusually long white line that develops after a decline

14. Please match the following patterns with the letters on the following chart.

    A. Piercing line _____

    B. Belt hold _____

    C. Window _____

    D. Harami _____

15. Please match the following patterns with the letters on the following chart:

    A. Harami _____

    B. Dark cloud cover _____

    C. Engulfing pattern _____

    D. Doji _____

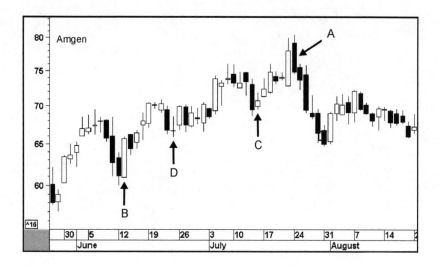

13
Candlesticks

Answers

1. **F.**

2. **D.** Candles also require the opening price. Since this was not available, it would not be possible to plot a correct candle chart so none of these patterns could be plotted.

3. **A.** Opening; **B.** closing

4. **C.** In an engulfing pattern the second real body totally engulfs the first. A piercing line is the bullish equivalent of a dark cloud cover.

5. **A.**

6. **Umbrella.**

7. **A** = Yes; **B** = Yes; **C** = Yes.

8. **D.**

9. **A.**

10. **B.**

11. **C.** A tweezer top requires the highs of two candles to be identical.

12. **D.**

13. **D.**

14. **A** = B; **B** = A; **C** = D; **D** = C

15. **A** = C; **B** = A; **C** = B; **D** = D

14
Point and Figure Charts

Questions

Subjects to Be Covered

Point and figure versus bar charts
Setting box amounts
Measuring objectives
Time as an element

1. How do bar charts and point and figure charts differ?
   A. Point and figure charts are plotted at specific time intervals.
   B. Point and figure charts record all time periods.
   C. Point and figure charts can never be plotted for intraday intervals.
   D. None of the above.

2. If a box is set at price movements of 5 points, this means that
   _____.
   A. All fluctuations less than 5 will be recorded.
   B. Only fluctuations greater than 5 will be plotted.
   C. Price fluctuations of 5 points will be recorded.
   D. None of the above.

3. Please fill in the blanks:

   In point and figure charts, _____ are plotted for rising prices and _____ for declining ones.

4. For stocks trading above $20, the accepted norm for a box is
   _____.
   A. 1 dollar
   B. 50 cents
   C. 5 dollars
   D. 2 dollars

5. Please fill in the blanks:

   When plotting a point and figure chart, there are two decisions to be made. The first is the (A) b_____ size and the second is whether to use a regular point and figure formula or a (B) r_____ chart.

6. A reversal chart in point and figure jargon is the same as a reversal pattern for bar charts.
   A. True
   B. False

7. Time is an important element in point and figure charting.
   A. Yes
   B. No

8. Please fill in the blanks:

   Measuring objectives for bar charts are achieved with a (A) v_____ count, but with point and figure it is done with a (B) h_____ count.

9. One disadvantage of point and figure charts is _____.
   A. They do not reflect support and resistance areas very well.
   B. Measuring objectives from irregular formations can be confusing to determine.
   C. They do not emphasize the amount of price swings that take place within a given price congestion zone.
   D. All of the above.

10. The smaller the box size, _____.
    A. The greater the number of price fluctuations
    B. The bigger the reversal amount should be
    C. The shorter the period that can be reasonably plotted and studied
    D. A and C

14
Point and Figure Charts

Answers

1. **D.** The principal difference is that point and figure charts ignore time. Time intervals are plotted at the base of point and figure charts merely to act as a reference point. They have no analytical significance.

2. **B.**

3. **Xs and Os.**

4. **A.**

5. **A.** box; **B.** reversal.

6. **B.** They are different. The reversal chart refers to a plotting technique; the reversal pattern is a price formation derived from any plotting technique, the completion of which signals a reversal in the prevailing trend.

7. **B.** Time is totally ignored in point and figure charting, though dates may be placed at the foot of the chart for reference purposes.

8. **A.** vertical; **B.** horizontal.

9. **B.** The other answers outline pluses for point and figure charting; for example, they do reflect support and resistance zones well.

10. **D.**

15

Miscellaneous Techniques for Determining Trends

Questions

Subjects to Be Covered

Support and resistance defined
Determining likely support/resistance points
Fibonacci fan lines
Techniques associated with proportion interpretation

1. Support is a concentration of supply sufficient to halt a rally temporarily.
    A. True
    B. False

2. Is the price likely to find resistance at the black line in the following chart if it falls any further?
    A. Yes
    B. No

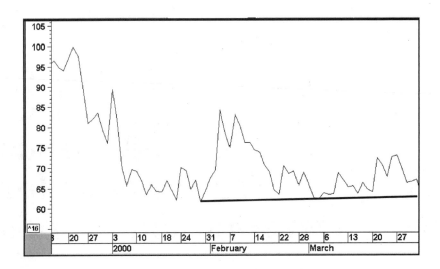

3. Name four technical characteristics as described in the text that could result in a support or resistance point.
   i.   Round numbers
   ii. Emotional points
   iii. Trendline reversals
   iv. Moderate overbought levels
   v.   Proportionate retracement and projection levels
   A. i, ii, v
   B. i, ii, iii, v
   C. i, ii, iii, iv, and v
   D. iv and v

4. A support/resistance area gains its significance from
_____.
   A. The amount of activity that develops at a specific point
   B. The speed of the previous move
   C. The number of people that were previously stopped out at that level
   D. A and B

5. Fill in the blanks:

(A) R_____ is a concentration of supply sufficient to temporarily halt an (B) a_____.

6. Fill in the blanks:

Support is a concentration of (A) s_____ sufficient to
(B) t_____ halt a decline.

7. Fill in the blank:

Proportionate moves are easier to spot on r_____ scaled charts.

8. Which of the following is not a Fibonacci number?
   A. 3
   B. 6
   C. 144
   D. 1

9. If the price falls back to a Fibonacci fan line, which course of action is legitimate?
   A. Buy, because it's a great opportunity.
   B. Consider buying, but also look at the other indicators.
   C. Go short if the line is penetrated.
   D. Consider going short if the line is penetrated, but review the other indicators before taking any action.
   E. B and D
   F. A and D

10. If the price retraces more than two-thirds of a rally, it's safe to conclude that the trend has reversed.
   A. True
   B. False

11. If the angle of a line from a pivotal point is 45 degrees and the chart measures price and time equally, what is the rise run ratio?
   A. 1×1
   B. 2×1
   C. 3×1
   D. 1×2

12. Who developed the idea of speed resistance lines?
   A. W. D. Gann
   B. Leonardo Fibonacci
   C. Leonardo Da Vinci
   D. Edson Gould

15
Miscellaneous Techniques for Determining Trends

Answers

1. **B.** The question defines resistance, not support.

2. **B.** No, it will find support. Support develops on the way down and resistance on the way up.

3. **B.**

4. **D.**

5. **A.** Resistance; **B.** advance.

6. **A.** supply; **B.** temporarily.

7. **ratio.**

8. **B.**

9. **E.** Fibonacci fan lines only represent an intelligent place to anticipate a reversal. Therefore, a review of other indicators is mandatory. When the line is penetrated, you can expect lower prices, but it is mandatory to review the other indicators. For example, the price may be oversold at that point and so on.

10. B. Sometimes a price will retrace 100 percent of a move and more. This does not in and of itself signal that the trend has reversed. The two-thirds retracement concept is merely a guideline to indicate that we should expect to see most retracements fall within the two-thirds rule.

11. A.

12. D. Edson Gould.

16

The Concept of Relative Strength

Questions

Subjects to Be Covered

What is relative strength?
Interpreting relative strength
Comparing the relative to the absolute price
Using trendlines with relative strength
Comparing the relative action of two different stock markets

1. Which of the following statements is true?
   A. Relative strength measures the relationship between two securities.
   B. The relationship between a stock and a market average is the only useful way of using relative strength.
   C. Comparative relative strength includes the RSI.
   D. A and B.

2. When the RS trend reverses to the downside, it is safe to conclude _____.
   A. That the price will sooner or later follow suite
   B. That it is probably a whipsaw since the price has not confirmed
   C. That you should be on the lookout for vulnerability in the stock because weakening RS often precedes a top in the absolute price
   D. None of the above

3. On the chart below, please draw a head-and-shoulders top on the RS line where the moving average is violated at approximately the same time as the neckline. An example (without the MA crossover) has already been constructed to offer you some guidance.

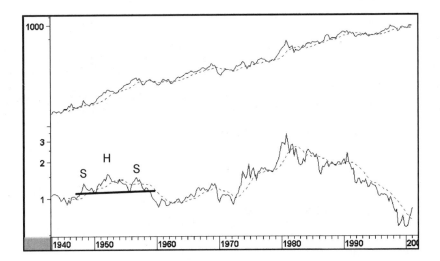

4. When a positive RS divergence develops, you should conclude

    _____.

    A. That the RS trend is now up and that it's safe to buy the stock
    B. Nothing
    C. That the technical position is improving, but you need to see more evidence of a trend reversal in the RS before buying the stock
    D. None of the above

5. On the following chart, please draw two trendlines between 1997 and 1999 that would have signaled a trend reversal in price and RS. Tip: One is a 4-year line and the other is a 2-year line.

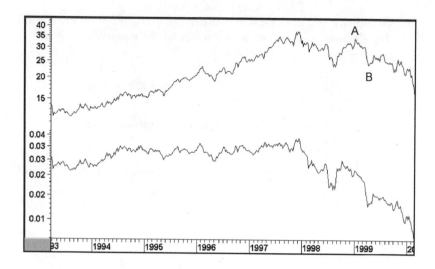

6. What was the piece of conclusive evidence that suggested the rally at A
in the following chart was going to fail?
  A. There was a declining series of peaks and troughs on the price.
  B. The RS has already been declining sharply.
  C. There was no strong evidence.

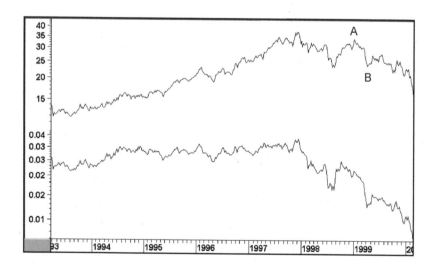

7. What price action suggested that the low in the absolute price at B in the previous chart would be taken out on the downside?
   A. The price was already falling.
   B. Gut feel.
   C. The RS line had already broken below its previous low.
   D. There is no evidence.

8. The price of corn is divided by the S&P Composite. Is this an RS relationship?
   A. Yes
   B. No, because one is a commodity, and the other is a market index

9. A strong uptrendline in the NASDAQ/S&P Ratio is violated and a head-and-shoulders top is completed. You should _____.
   A. Buy the NASDAQ.
   B. Sell the NASDAQ.
   C. Buy the S&P.
   D. Sell the S&P.
   E. Short the NASDAQ and buy the S&P.
   F. Short the S&P and buy the NASDAQ.

10. If the RS line for the FTSE breaks out against the World Stock Index but that for the Swedish market does not, which is the better buy based on this relationship alone?
    A. The FTSE
    B. The Swedish Index
    C. The World Index
    D. None of the above

16
The Concept of
Relative Strength

Answers

1. **A.** Comparative relative strength should never be confused with the
    relative strength indicator. There are other useful ways of applying RS
    apart from comparing a stock to a market average.

2. **C.**

3. **The answer is shown in the chart.**

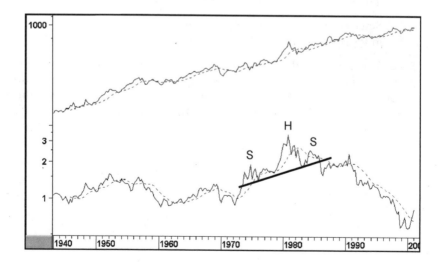

4. **D.** This is correct because you need to see more evidence that the RS has turned, but more importantly, evidence that the stock itself is now in an uptrend.

5. **The answer is shown in the chart.**

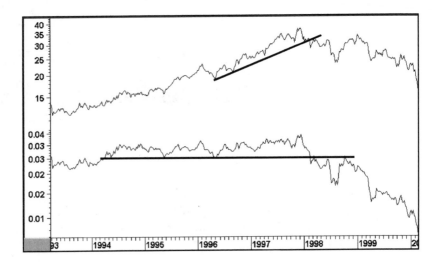

6. **C.** The declining RS was evidence but not conclusive evidence.

7. **C.** The RS line was already below its previous trough.

8. **A.** Since comparative RS compares one security with another, this is a valid RS relationship.

9. **E.** There is no evidence that either of the components has reversed trend; therefore, choices A through D are not appropriate. Since the break indicates that the S&P will now outperform the NASDAQ, the S&P should be bought and the NASDAQ shorted.

10. **A.**

18
Price: The Major Averages

Questions

Subjects to Be Covered

Types of averages and indexes
DJ Utilities and their relationship with the industrials
The Value Line and a market indicator
Nature of the Russell Indexes

1. The S&P Composite is an unweighted index.
   A. True
   B. False

2. The DJIA _____.
   A. Is a composite index
   B. Is a measure of 30 different stocks from all the principle industries
   C. Uses a divisor in its calculation
   D. All of the above

3. Please fill in the blanks:

   The DJ Utility Average is (A) i_____ sensitive. This means that it often (B) l_____ the industrials.

4. Which moving average did William Gordon use in his calculation for the DJIA?
   A. 25-week
   B. 12-month
   C. 45-week
   D. 40-week

5. Why is the relationship between the DJIA and the DJ Utilities often overlooked?
   A. Because it doesn't work very well
   B. Because there is usually a lot of excitement elsewhere when they are diverging
   C. Because GM is a better indicator
   D. All of the above

6. If the Value Line Arithmetic diverges negatively with the S&P Composite, _____.
   A. Be on the lookout for a decline when the S&P confirms with a trend break.
   B. Sell immediately.
   C. Buy the S&P because it has superior relative strength.
   D. Ignore the whole thing.

7. General Motors _____.
   A. Has a habit of leading the market at tops and bottoms
   B. Tends to lead at tops, but is inconsistent at bottoms
   C. Is sensitive to interest rates and credit availability
   D. A and B
   E. B and C

8. Please fill in the blanks:

   In 2001 the Russell (A) _____ consisted of 98 percent of the investable stock value in the (B) _____. The Russell (C) _____ contains the largest blue chips and the Russell (D) _____ is often used as a proxy for low-cap stocks.

9. Which is the most comprehensive average?
   A. The DJIA
   B. The Russell 3000
   C. The S&P Composite
   D. The Wilshire 5000

10. What year were the DJ Rails renamed the DJ Transports?
    A. 1987
    B. 1898
    C. 1970
    D. 1955

18
Price: The Major Averages

Answers

1. **B.** The S&P is weighted by capitalization.

2. **C.** The DJIA excludes utilities and transports and is not therefore a composite index.

3. **A.** interest; **B.** leads.

4. **D.**

5. **B.**

6. **A.** The divergence warns that the technical position is suspect, but requires a confirmation from the S&P in the form of a trend-reversal signal before you can make a final conclusion that the odds favor a decline.

7. **E.** One of the reasons GM leads at market tops is because it is partially interest-rate sensitive, since the level of rates has a big influence on financing and leasing cost and therefore the public's ability to purchase autos.

8. **A.** 3000; **B.** United States; **C.** 1000; **D.** 2000.

9. **D.**

10. **C.**

19

Group Rotation

Questions

Subjects to Be Covered

Characteristics of liquidity-driven groups
Characteristics of earnings-driven groups
The individual groups that fall under liquidity- and earnings-driven groups

1. Since the business cycle moves from an inflationary to a deflationary part, groups sensitive to inflationary conditions have a tendency to lead the market.
   A. True
   B. False

2. Which of the following statements is true?
   A. Inflation-sensitive groups do well when interest rates are declining.
   B. Occasionally, unusual fundamentals for a group will override the normal rotational process.
   C. Liquidity-driven groups do well when commodity prices are rising sharply.
   D. None of the above.

3. Please fill in the blanks:

   Steels often bottom out at the same time as the S&P Composite, but they tend to put in their best relative performance at the (A) e_____ of the cycle. Electric utilities have a tendency to (B) l_____ the S&P at market tops.

4. Which of the following fall under the term of *liquidity*-driven groups?
   A. Steels, papers, chemicals, and insurance companies
   B. Retailers, computers, and oils

   C. Utilities, tobacco, soft drinks, and property casualty insurers
   D. None of the above

5. Which of the following fall under the term of *earnings*-driven groups?
   A. Mines, oils, and chemicals
   B. Steels, retailers, and personal care
   C. Papers, mines, and electric utilities
   D. Electric utilities, life insurers, and retailers

6. If the technical position indicated a switch favoring inflation-sensitive groups, it is OK to buy _____.
   A. Mines
   B. Brokers
   C. Insurance
   D. None of the above

7. If the market is peaking, which groups are probably already in bear markets?
   A. Mines
   B. Oils
   C. Electric utilities
   D. Insurance companies
   E. C and D

19
Group Rotation

Answers

1. **B.** It is the deflation- or liquidity-sensitive groups that lead the market at bottoms, not the inflation- or earnings-driven groups.

2. **B.** Sometimes specific changes in the fundamentals will cause it to move out of sequence.

3. **A.** End; **B.** lead.

4. **C.**

5. **A.**

6. **D.** It's only OK to buy a group when its technical position is positive. This is usually the case when the environment is inflationary, but not necessarily so.

7. **E.**

20

Time: Longer-Term Cycles

Questions

Subjects to Be Covered

Knowledge of cycle lengths and names
Characteristics of cycles
Principles, such as summation and variation
Seasonal patterns

1. Please match the following:
   A. Juglar _____ A. 50- to 54-year cycle
   B. Kitchen _____ B. Business cycles
   C. Kondratieff _____ C. 41-month cycle
   D. Edward Dewey _____ D. 9.2-year cycle
   E. Joseph Schumpeter _____ E. Decenniel cycle
   F. Edgar Lawrence Smith _____ F. Foundation for the study of cycles

2. Please fill in the blanks:

   Time is concerned with (A) a_____, because the (B) l_____ a trend takes to complete, the greater its psychological acceptance and the greater the necessity for prices to move in the (C) o_____ direction and adjust accordingly.

3. Please fill in the blanks:

Prices move in periodic fluctuations known as (A) c_____.
(B) C_____ can operate for periods ranging from a few days to
many decades. At any given moment a number of (C) c_____
are operating simultaneously, and since they are exerting different
forces at different times, the interaction of their changing
relationships often has the effect of distorting the timing of
a particular (D) c_____.

4. The principle of variation states that while stocks go through similar
cycles, the price magnitudes and durations of these nominal cycles
will be different because of fundamental and psychological
considerations.
   A. True
   B. False

5. A magnitude failure _____.
   A. Occurs in a bull market where a cyclic high develops below its
      predecessor
   B. Occurs in a bear market where a cyclic high develops below its
      predecessor
   C. Both A and B
   D. Neither A nor B

6. When a number of cycles are combined into one, this is known as the
principle of s_____.

7. Please match these answers:
   A. The most bearish   _____   A. Years ending in a 5
      month based on
      percent gain or loss
   B. The most bullish   _____   B. September
      month based on
      percent gain or loss
   C. The most bullish year   _____   C. Monday
   D. The most bearish year   _____   D. December
   E. One of the most bullish _____   E. The last 2 days of the old
      times of the month   month and the first 3 days
                                           of the new month
   F. The most bearish   _____   F. Years ending in a 7
      day of the week

8. Recognizing that all cycles fail from time to time, which has proved to be the most reliable?
A. The Kondratieff wave
B. The 18-year cycle
C. The 9.2-year cycle
D. The 4-year cycle

9. Preholiday trading sessions tend to be bullish for equities. Which was the most bullish between 1963 and 1982?
A. President's day
B. Thanksgiving day
C. Independence day
D. Christmas day

10. Research between 1897 and 1986 has shown that the 4 days preceding the third trading session of a new month offer superior returns than the average trading day.
A. You can buy on the last trading day and cash in on the third day of the new month.
B. Look at the position of the short-term oscillators before making a trade.
C. A and B.
D. Use this as one indicator in the weight of the evidence approach.

20
Time: Longer-Term Cycles

Answers

1. **A** = D; **B** = C; **C** = A; **D** = F; **E** = B; **F** = E.

2. **A.** Adjustment; **B.** longer; **C.** opposite.

3. **A.** Cycles; **B.** cycles; **C.** cycles; **D.** cycle.

4. **A.**

5. **A.** Answer B is a normal phenomenon in a bear market where it is expected that each succeeding peak will be lower than its predecessor. This is not expected in a bull market, hence the expression failure.

6. **Summation.**

7. **A** = B; **B** = D; **C** = A; **D** = F; **E** = E; **F** = C.

8. **D.**

9. **B.**

10. **D.** This is just one indicator. You should also look at the position of other indicators, such as oscillators, before making a decision.

21

Practical Identification of Cycles

Questions

Subjects to Be Covered

Cycles defined
How the timing of cycle peaks indicates strength or weakness
The importance of a confluence of cycles
Integrating cycles with other technical tools

1. Please fill in the blank:

   A c_____ is a recognizable price pattern or movement that occurs with some degree of regularity in a specific time period.

2. Successive lows that are higher or lower than their predecessor are of great importance in identifying cycles.
   A. True
   B. False

3. Please fill in the blanks:

   When the cycle high develops shortly after the cycle low, the implications are that the upward part of the cycle is (A) w_____ and that its overall strength lies on the (B) d_____. In this situation, each cycle low is normally (C) l_____ than that of its predecessor.

4. A cycle high that is "late" in arriving, that is, that arrives well after the halfway point of the idealized cycle is _____.
   A. Likely to reflect a stronger-than-average rally
   B. Likely to be developing in a bear market

C. Will be followed by a sharp correction to catch up with the bearish side of the cycle
D. All of the above
E. None of the above

5. When a cycle high develops at the time when a low is expected, the cycle is said to be _____.
A. Broken
B. Invalid
C. Inverted
D. Inadvertent

6. Which of the following are incorrect statements?
A. The more cycles that are bottoming simultaneously, the more significant the low is likely to be.
B. The longer the cycle, the greater its significance.
C. It is possible to observe cyclic highs that develop at regular intervals.
D. None of the above

7. Which of the following statements are correct?
A. Cycles should always be used in conjunction with other indicators.
B. Cycles should only be used with oscillators.
C. Cyclic highs that develop halfway along a cycle are perfect.
D. None of the above.

21

Practical Identification of Cycles

Answers

1. **Cycle.**

2. **B.** It is the distance between the lows that are important, not their level.

3. **A.** weak; **B.** downside; **C.** lower. Substitute words that have the same meaning that are acceptable as answers—for example, soft for weak, below for lower, and so on.

4. **A.** Cycle highs that are late in arriving are usually a sign of a very strong trend.

5. **C.**

6. **D.** All these statements are correct.

7. **A.** Cycles are just another technical tool and as such are far from perfect. It therefore makes sense to always use them in conjunction with other indicators.

22
Volume Principles

Questions

Subjects to Be Covered

Volume characteristics in rising trends
Volume characteristics in falling trends
Volume characteristics at turning points

1. Based on current trends of volume and price, shown in the following chart, what is likely to happen next in terms of the next major move?
   A. The price will rise.
   B. The price will consolidate.
   C. The price will soon fall.
   D. The price is guaranteed to fall.

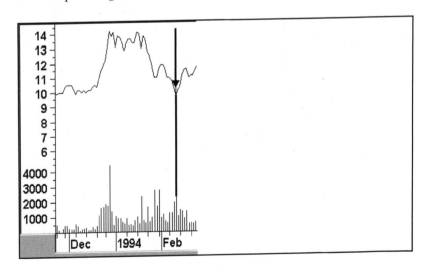

2. In all situations when the price rises and volume falls, this is bearish.
   A. True
   B. False

3. Which is generally the strongest and more reliable signal?
   A. A selling climax
   B. Record volume
   C. Declining volume
   D. Rising volume

4. What is likely to happen next in the chart below?
   A. The price will rally.
   B. The price will decline.
   C. A trading range.
   D. None of the above.

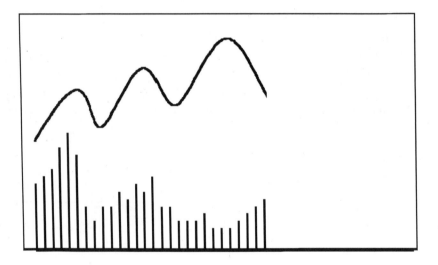

5. Which is the normal situation?
   A. Volume goes with the trend.
   B. Volume leads price.
   C. Volume contracts when prices decline.
   D. All of the above.

6. If the price rises and volume contracts and then the price falls and volume expands, _____.
   A. This is bearish.
   B. This is bullish.
   C. This is normal action.
   D. There is no indication of whether this is bullish or bearish.

7. When a rally culminates in a parabolic blowoff of volume, it is _____.
   A. A certain sign of a top
   B. A sign of exhaustion and therefore the odds favor a top
   C. A sign that one more rally to a new high on low volume should be expected
   D. None of the above

22
Volume Principles

Answers

1. **C.** When volume falls and the price rises, the trend is suspect and usually results in a decline. Although the odds favor this outcome, there is certainly no guarantee that this will happen. The following chart shows the answer.

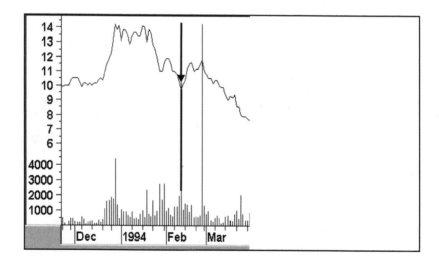

2. **B.** Most of the time this is a correct statement. However, when the price rises from a selling climax on falling volume this is normal. Since selling climaxes are normally bullish, this represents an exception. Also, we find situations in the charts when the rising price/falling volume rule does not work, even though this is the norm.

3. **B.** While not a perfect indicator, record volume is usually a strong and reliable signal.

4. **B.** This is because the price is falling under a trend of rising volume, which is a bearish characteristic.

5. **D.**

6. **A.** Rising price and falling volume is abnormal and bearish. So too is declining price and expanding volume.

7. **B.** A parabolic blowoff is normally associated with a top. Since it is an exhaustion characteristic it is highly unlikely that a new high would be seen immediately after the blowoff. **A** is wrong because there are no certainties in technical analysis.

23

Volume Indicators

Questions

Subjects to Be Covered

Interpreting the rate of change of volume
The calculation and interpretation of the Demand Index
The assumptions underlying the calculation of the Chaikin Money Flow
Interpreting the Chaikin Money Flow
Construction and interpretation of the Arms Index

1. A high reading in a volume ROC indicates _____.
   A. A high level of volume
   B. An overbought market
   C. An oversold market
   D. A and B

2. What is likely to happen when both trendlines in the following chart are violated?
   A. The price will rally.
   B. The price will fall.
   C. The price will move sideways.
   D. There is not information to make a reliable forecast.

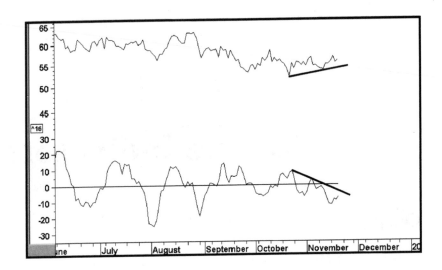

3. When the volume oscillator reaches a peak and starts to reverse, this
   indicates _____.
   A. A top
   B. A bottom
   C. A probable trend reversal
   D. None of the above

4. Volume usually leads price during rallies.
   A. True
   B. False

5. The Demand Index combines price and volume into one indicator.
   A. True
   B. False

6. A high reading in the Demand Index indicates _____.
   A. An overbought or oversold condition with the price
   B. An overbought condition
   C. An oversold condition
   D. A and C

7. The Demand Index is interpreted _____.
   A. Using overbought/oversold levels
   B. With trendline breaks
   C. Using divergence analysis
   D. All of the above

8. What does the Chaikin Money Flow assume in its calculation?
   A. That prices close near their low on decreasing volume at the end of a rally
   B. That prices close near their high at the end of a decline on rising volume
   C. That prices close near their high on rising volume in an advance and near their low on rising volume during a decline
   D. None of the above

9. What is the strongest interpretive technique for the Chaikin Money Flow as described in the text?
   A. Moving average analysis
   B. Overbought/oversold crossovers
   C. Trendline analysis
   D. Divergences

10. On balance volume is best interpreted with _____.
   A. Overbought/oversold conditions
   B. Divergences
   C. Trendline analysis
   D. B and C
   E. A, B, and C

11. What statements are true of the Arms Index?
   A. It moves inversely with price.
   B. It is constructed from volume and breadth data.
   C. A reading in the 10-day series in excess of 1.5 is bearish.
   D. A and B.
   E. A, B, and C.

23
Volume Indicators

Answers

1. **A.** A high reading merely indicates a high level of volume. This could come during a rally or a decline.

2. **B.** When the price falls and volume rises, this is bearish.

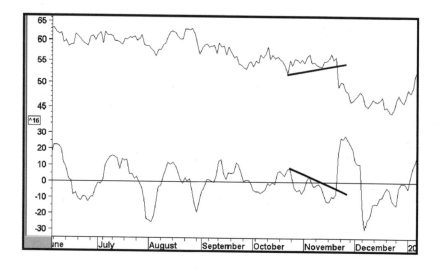

3. **C.** A peaking in the oscillator indicates a probable exhaustion move in volume, which is often followed by a trend reversal.

4. **A.** Volume can coincide with price, but usually leads it. Rarely does volume lag the price.

5. **A.**

6. **B.** The Demand Index, unlike the volume ROC and oscillator, always moves in the same direction as the price.

7. **D.**

8. **C.**

9. **D.** All of the above are legitimate interpretive techniques, but the strongest characteristic of this indicator is its ability to point up divergences.

10. **D.** The OBV is not an oscillator and does not experience overbought/oversold conditions.

11. **D.** A reading in excess of 1.5 is bullish, not bearish.

24
Breadth

Questions

Subjects to Be Covered

Methods of A/D line construction
Interpretation of breadth indicators
The concept of diffusion indicators and their interpretation
The concept of seasonal momentum and its interpretation
The concept of net new highs
The McClellan oscillator and Summation Index

1. What are the ways in which an A/D line can be calculated?
   A. By cumulating the daily plurality of advances and declines
   B. By cumulating the difference between advances and declines divided by the number of unchanged
   C. By cumulating the daily difference between the daily new highs and lows
   D. A and B

2. What is the most common method for interpreting the A/D line?
   A. Overbought/oversold conditions
   B. Divergences
   C. Reverse price patterns
   D. A and C

3. Advance decline lines can be constructed for any market that contains a basket of components.
   A. True
   B. False

4. Before using any A/D line for comparative purposes, it is first necessary to _____.

    A. Calculate an EMA.

    B. Plot it with an oscillator.

    C. Calculate winter momentum.

    D. Check to see if the line has a historical downward bias.

5. Please fill in the blanks:

Breadth data may be expressed as an Advance/Decline (A) l_____ or an (B) o_____. Both forms may be used to identify positive and negative (C) d_____.

6. Which description best describes how the McClellan oscillator is calculated?

    A. From advancing less declining issues

    B. By comparing two simple moving averages

    C. By comparing two EMAs of the daily A/D line for a specific market

    D. By calculating a smoothed ROC of an A/D line

7. Which, if any, are correct statements if the McClellan oscillator is above zero?

    A. The Summation Index will also be above zero.

    B. The Summation Index will be rising.

    C. The Summation Index will be above its MA.

    D. None of the above.

8. The A/D line tends to lead the market at peaks because _____.

    A. Many issues are interest sensitive and interest rates lead equities.

    B. Market participants tend to lose confidence in smaller companies before large ones and there are more small companies.

    C. Because they all have a downward bias.

    D. A and B.

9. In using the concept of seasonal momentum, a high and reversing level in which season often signals major buying opportunities?

    A. Winter

    B. Spring

    C. Summer

    D. Fall

10. Please fill in the blank:

A d_____ indicator measures the percentage of a basket of securities that are experiencing a positive trend.

11. Please fill in the blanks:

Under the concept of seasonal momentum major declines are sometimes avoided when (A) f_____ moves into (B) s_____ instead of to winter. This is known as an (C) I_____
(D) s_____.

12. Which is a better bell weather for the broad market?
A. The A/D line
B. The DJIA
C. The S&P Composite
D. The NASDAQ Composite

13. The net new high data should always be calculated with a 52-week time span.
A. True
B. False

14. Please fill in the blanks:

A new high indicator based on the (A) c_____ plurality of daily net new high data is a useful addition to the breadth indicator family. The text suggests that it can usefully be used with (B) a _____ -day MA to signal bullish and bearish environments.

24
Breadth

Answers

1. **D.** There are actually several other ways in which the line can be calculated, but these are the two most common.

2. **B.** There are many ways to interpret A/D lines such as trendline violations, price pattern completions, and MA crossovers, but the most common is divergences, both negative and positive. There is no such thing as a reverse price pattern.

3. **A.**

4. **D.**

5. **A.** line; **B.** oscillator; **C.** divergences

6. **C.**

7. **B.** If the oscillator is above zero, it will add to the total for the Summation Index, which means that it will be rising. The Index itself could be above or below zero.

8. **D.** Some, but not all, A/D lines have a downward bias.

9. **A.**

10. **Diffusion.**

11. **A.** fall; **B.** summer; **C.** Indian; **D.** summer.

12. **A.**

13. **B.** 52 weeks has been the traditional measure, but there is no reason why any realistic time period cannot be used.

14. **A.** cumulative; **B.** 100.

25
Interest Rates and the Stock Market

Questions

Subjects to Be Covered

The relationship between interest rates and equity prices
The three-step-and-stumble rule
Credit market sectors

1. Which is more important as an influence on the economy and equity prices?
   A. The level of short-term rates
   B. The level of long-term rates
   C. The rate of change of short-term rates
   D. The rate of change of long-term rates

2. Changes in the primary trend of short-term interest rates have led every stock market bottom since 1921.
   A. True
   B. False

3. Changes in interest rates have an influence on stock prices because _____.
   A. Credit market instruments represent competition for equity money.
   B. Stocks are often bought on margin, and changes in the cost of margin affect buying and selling decisions.
   C. Changes in interest rates affect the level of economic activity and therefore indirectly affect corporate profits.
   D. A, B, and C.

4. Was the answer to the previous question a complete list as indicated in the text?
   A. Yes
   B. No

5. Please match the following: (for example, A = C)
   A. The long end of the   _____ A. Money market instruments
      bond market
   B. A maturity of a year   _____ B. A maturity of at least 10 years
      or less
   C. Intermediate maturities _____ C. A maturity falling between 1
                                           and 10 years

6. Please fill in the blanks:

   Federal funds, 3-month eurodollars, and 3-month T-bills are all
   (A) m_____ m_____ instruments. The (B) F_____
   R_____ has a greater influence over these sectors than over
   long-term (C) i_____ r_____.

7. Changes in the gold price are a perfect indicator for predicting changes in bond yields.
   A. True
   B. False

8. If a short-term oscillator fails to reach an overbought condition over a period of several months and oversold conditions fail to signal a rally, this indicates _____.
   A. A primary bull market environment
   B. A primary bear market environment
   C. A or B
   D. None of the above

9. The three-step-and-stumble rule states _____.
   A. That if the discount rate had been raised three times, the top in the stock market has been seen
   B. That if the discount rate has been raised three times, we should expect equity prices to immediately stumble
   C. That if the discount rate has been raised three times, the clock has begun to tick for the bull market in equities
   D. That if the discount rate has been lowered three times, stock prices are likely to stumble

10. Please fill in the blanks:

   The three main sectors in the U.S. bond market are (A) t_____
   e_____, (B) c_____, and (C) g_____.

25

Interest Rates and the Stock Market

Answers

1. **C.**

2. **B.** Interest rates almost always lead stock market bottoms, but there are rare exceptions, such as 1987. Since this was not associated with a recession, it could be argued that the relationship did not fall into the norm. However, the 1987 crash did meet the magnitude qualification for a bear market.

3. **D.**

4. **B.** Changes in rates also affect the cost of capital and therefore affect corporate profits directly.

5. **A** = B; **B** = A; **C** = C.

6. **A.** money market; **B.** Federal Reserve; **C.** interest rates.

7. **B.** Gold discounts inflationary trends and is therefore a useful indicator, but it is far from perfect.

8. **B.**

9. **C.** Once the rate has been raised three times, the market becomes vulnerable, but the leads in each cycle have varied considerably in each cycle since the inauguration of the Federal Reserve.

10. **A.** tax exempt; **B.** corporate; **C.** government.

26
Market Sentiment

Questions

Subjects to Be Covered

Differentiating between savvy and less-smart groups of market participants
Interpretation of sentiment indicators
Substitutes for sentiment indicators

1. Which of the following tend to act in a manner contrary to that of the majority?
    A. Market letter writers
    B. Traders
    C. Specialists
    D. Insiders
    E. All of the above
    F. C and D

2. Why is it probable that short interest numbers have become distorted?
    A. Because of the big bull market in the 1980s and 1990s.
    B. Because of the advent of futures and options, which increases arbitrage opportunities.
    C. It's easy to short now more than ever.
    D. None of the above.

3. A short interest ratio in excess of 1.8 is always bullish.
    A. True
    B. False

4. When 90 percent of market letter writers are bearish, this is bullish.
    A. True
    B. False

5. Which of the following statements is true?
   A. The trend of sentiment can be just as important as the level.
   B. All sentiment indicators are distorted and therefore should be used sparingly.
   C. Trendline violations in sentiment indicators occasionally give good buy and sell signals.
   D. None of the above.
   E. A and C.

6. Please fill in the blank:

   When sentiment indicators are not available, it is possible to substitute m_____ indicators since both series reflect mood changes in traders and investors.

7. Which is more likely to offer the stronger signal?
   A. An extremely low Market Vane bond bull reading in a bear market
   B. An extremely high Market Vane bond bull reading in a bear market
   C. An extremely high Market Vane bullish bond reading in a bull market
   D. B and C

8. When the level of margin debt crosses below its 12-month EMA, this is usually _____.
   A. Bullish
   B. Bearish

9. An extreme reading in the Market Vane bullish bond numbers is usually associated with _____.
   A. A short or intermediate turning point
   B. A primary trend turning point

10. Mutual fund cash/asset ratios are _____.
    A. Sentiment indicators
    B. Flow of funds indicators
    C. Oscillators
    D. A and B

26
Market Sentiment

Answers

1. **F.**

2. **B.**

3. **B.** This used to be the case, but in recent decades numbers well in excess of 1.8 have been registered.

4. **A.** Market letter writers are contrary indicators.

5. **E.** When they do, it is always a good idea to get some kind of trend confirmation signal from the price itself.

6. **Momentum.**

7. **B.** Contratrend signals are usually more powerful than protrend signals. Bearish (a low number of bulls) readings in a bear market do not necessarily generate strong rallies, whereas a large number of bulls in a bear market are likely to be followed by a strong decline.

8. **B.** When margin debt is contracting, this indicates a lack of confidence and is bearish.

9. **A.** Because this is a short-term indicator, it signals less important turning points.

10. **D.** These indicators can be used as flow of funds or sentiment indicators.

27
Applying Technical Analysis to Contrary Opinion

Questions

Subjects to Be Covered

Contrary opinion defined
Personalities who have written about crowd psychology
Steps in forming a contrary opinion
Why it is difficult to go contrary

1. Please fill in the blanks:

   The guiding light of investment contrarianism is not that the majority view—the conventional or received wisdom—is always wrong. Rather it's that the majority opinion tends to solidify into a (A) d_____ while its basic premises begin to lose their original (B) v_____ and so become progressively more (C) m _____ in the marketplace.

2. As described in the text, the three steps to forming a contrary opinion might include _____.
   A. Reading popular magazines and jotting down notes
   B. Figuring out what the crowd thinks
   C. Talking to your friends
   D. Determining when the crowd reaches an extreme
   E. Forming alternative scenarios
   F. B, D, and E
   G. A, D, and E
   H. A, B, and E

3. Please fill in the blanks:

When the (A) c_____ reaches an extreme, the question is not
(B) w_____, but (C) w_____ and by (D) h_____ much.

4. Please match the following:

A. Gustav   _____   A. John
B. Mackay   _____   B. Charles
C. Humphrey _____   C. Le Bon
D. Schultz   _____   D. Neil

5. When you see several bullish cover stories and the price has risen
significantly over the previous 2 years, it is safe to buy.
A. True
B. False

6. Which of the following are reasons why it is difficult to go contrary?
A. Because most of us have a need to conform.
B. There is a certain comfort gained by heeding the advice of an
expert.
C. We tend to believe that the establishment has all the answers.
D. Because of the fear of being ridiculed.
E. All of the above.
F. A, B, and C.
G. A, B, and D.

27
Applying Technical Analysis to Contrary Opinion

Answers

1. **A.** Dogma; **B.** validity; **C.** mispriced.

2. **F.**

3. **A.** Crowd; **B.** whether; **C.** when; **D.** how.

4. **A** = C; **B** = B; **C** = D; **D** = A.

5. **B.** The crowd can sometimes move to an extreme, well beyond anyone's wildest expectations. Therefore, it is better to make sure that this is confirmed by a technical signal.

6. **E.**

29
Mechanical Trading Systems

Questions

Subjects to Be Covered

Advantages and disadvantages of mechanical systems
Appraising systems
Troubleshooting poorly performing systems

1. Mechanical systems are used as a substitute for judgment and thinking.
   A. True
   B. False

2. Which is likely to be a better system?
   A. One that has a perfect fit with historical data with one security
   B. One that has been consistently profitable but has an imperfect historical fit over many securities
   C. One that has a huge profit based on one or two signals
   D. None of the above

3. What are some of the advantages of well-designed mechanical systems?
   A. They remove objectivity.
   B. They remove subjectivity.
   C. They enable the trader to participate in every worthwhile move.
   D. A and C.
   E. B and C.

4. What are the disadvantages of automated systems?
   A. Backtesting won't necessarily simulate what actually would have happened.
   B. Random events can jeopardize a badly conceived system.
   C. There will be long periods when the best systems fail.
   D. All of the above.

5. If a buy signal is given, but there is no countervailing sell system, what is the problem?
   A. You are using too much margin.
   B. The system was not properly backtested.
   C. The system has not been designed precisely.
   D. The results were not extrapolated before entering the marketplace.
   E. B and D.

6. If you trade a proven and well-designed system and you lose all of your capital executing it, what is the problem likely to be?
   A. You do not have the aptitude to trade.
   B. You did not follow every signal without question.
   C. You did not make sure that you had enough capital to survive the worst losing streak during the test period.
   D. B and C.

7. Please fill in the blank:

   The worst string of losses from a specific open equity peak is known as the greatest d_____.

8. Looking at the equity curves from three different systems in the following chart, which one is likely to offer the best results?

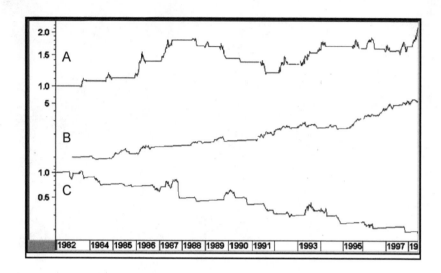

9. Which statement is true?
   A. If you don't invent enough rules, the sample data will not be profitable, and neither will the real-time application.
   B. The size of the drawdown is unimportant if the system is really profitable.
   C. If your system starts out a big winner in real-time, you know you've got it made.
   D. None of the above.

10. Using leverage with mechanical systems will _____.
    A. Always result in bigger gains for systems that test profitably
    B. Exaggerate the results both on the upside and downside
    C. Depend on the chronological sequence in which the gains and losses are, but will definitely exaggerate, the results both on the upside and downside
    D. Bust the account

29
Mechanical Trading Systems

Answers

1. **B.** You still have to do the thinking when designing and testing systems. They should also be re-appraised on a regular basis.

2. **B.**

3. **E.**

4. **D.**

5. **C.**

6. **D.**

7. **Drawdown.**

8. **B.** This line in the following chart has a consistent ring trend. A is too volatile and C loses money.

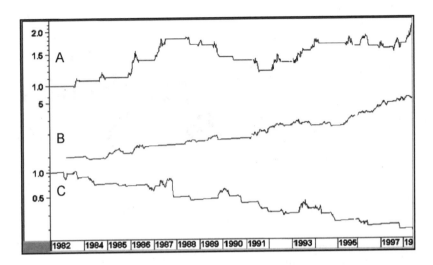

9. **D.**

10. **C.**

30

Technical Analysis of Global Markets

Questions

Subjects to Be Covered

The international 4-year cycle
Choice of World Indexes
Applying breadth indicators to the global equity scene

1. Which years represented a bottom in the 4-year business cycle?
   A. 1972, 1976, 1980, and 1984
   B. 1981, 1985, 1986, and 1992
   C. 1982, 1986, 1990, and 1995
   D. 1986, 1990, 1994, and 1998

2. The 4-year global stock cycle _____.
   A. Repeats exactly every 4 years
   B. Repeats approximately every 4 years
   C. Has worked consistently well since the 1960s, so it is guaranteed to work in the future
   D. B and C

3. Which is an incorrect statement?
   A. All markets move in the same direction all the time.
   B. Diffusion indexes cannot be used with the World Index because there is not enough data.
   C. The MSCI World Index is the only one worth using.
   D. A, B, and C.

4. The MSCI World Stock Index is weighted by market capitalization.
   A. True
   B. False

5. Based on the text, which are legitimate ways to interpret diffusion
   indicators constructed from a basket of individual country indexes?
   A. Divergence analysis
   B. Trendline analysis
   C. Relative action
   D. Overbought/oversold analysis
   E. A, B, and C
   F. A, B, and D
   G. A, B, C, and D

6. If fewer country indexes are making new highs as the World Index is
   rallying, what would you expect to happen?
   A. The World Index will decline.
   B. This is a negative sign but not a signal to sell until the World Index
      confirms with a negative trend reversal signal.
   C. The Index will rally.
   D. None of the above.

30
Technical Analysis of Global Markets

Answers

1. D.
2. B.
3. D.
4. A.
5. F. Relative action was not discussed in the text.
6. B.

31
Technical Analysis of Individual Stocks

Questions

Subjects to Be Covered

Ownership stages of stocks
The importance of the secular trend
Relating relative to absolute price trends
Relating individual stocks to industry groups
Using ratios of early to late cycle groups

1. Please fill in the blanks:

When a stock has risen sharply in price, bullish news is widespread and the media has fallen in love with it, the stock is said to be (A) o_____. When the opposite circumstances are present, the stock is said to be (B) u_____.

2. Which stocks best lend themselves to the buy-hold approach?
   A. Cyclicals
   B. Growth stocks
   C. Stocks with high betas
   D. All of the above

3. A secular price trend _____.
   A. Is a deeply religious one
   B. Lasts from 1 to 2 years
   C. Lasts over several business cycles
   D. Is more important than a primary trend
   E. B and D
   F. C and D

4. Stocks can be selected when the overall market conditions are right, the group looks positive, and the individual stock looks attractive, especially against the group. This approach is called the t_____ d_____ approach.

5. When the secular trend of the relative strength line reverses, but the uptrend in the absolute price trend is still intact, what is the best strategy?
   A. Hold on until the secular trend for the absolute price reverses.
   B. Sell and move into cash.
   C. Provided the overall market conditions are positive, switch to a stock with a positive absolute and relative price trend that are not overextended.
   D. None of the above.

6. Looking at the following chart, is it reasonable to anticipate a long-term KST buy signal?
   A. Yes
   B. No

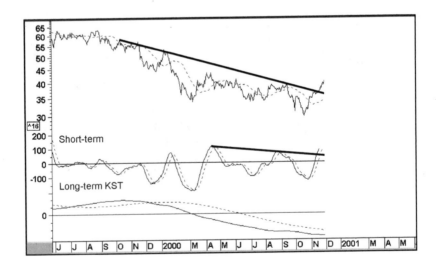

7. If the market and industry group have both turned positive, it is likely that some stocks in the group will outperform the others, but it is OK to buy any of them.
   A. True
   B. False

8. A ratio, such as the aluminum/banks, indicates that the cycle has moved to an inflationary stage.
   A. This means that it is OK to buy late-cycle leaders.
   B. This means that it is OK to buy early-cycle leaders provided their technical condition is solid.
   C. This means that it is OK to buy late-cycle leaders provided their technical condition is sound.
   D. Early- and mid-cycle leaders should not be bought under any circumstances.
   E. C and D.

9. If a stock is overowned, it should be immediately shorted.
   A. True
   B. False

10. When the stock market rallies off a bear market low, it is safe to buy any stock.
   A. True
   B. False

31
Technical Analysis of Individual Stocks

Answers

1. **A.** Overowned; **B.** underowned.

2. **B.**

3. **F.** The secular trend lasts for several business cycles and is more dominant than the primary trend because it lasts longer.

4. **The top-down.**

5. **C.** It's OK to hold on until the absolute price trend reverses, but better results will come from switching to a stock where the RS trend is positive.

6. **A.** Because the short-term KST has violated a downtrendline and the price has broken above a 1-year downtrendline.

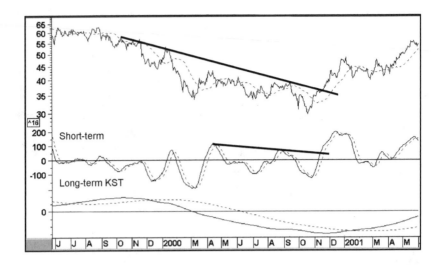

7. **B.** Each stock must be appraised on its own merits. The top-down approach is used merely as a short-cut filtering mechanism.

8. **C.** In general, it is better to stay with the late-cycle leaders since the probabilities favor their fortunes. However, there may be special circumstances why some other groups can outperform the market. Provided their technical position is sound, there is no reason why they cannot be purchased.

9. **B.** The stock may remain overowned for some time before it reverses. It should only be shorted when the technical position warrants such action.

10. **B.** It is never safe to buy any stock. Each issue must be analyzed on its own merits.

Index

About the Author

Martin J. Pring is the highly respected president of Pring Research (**www.pring.com**) editor of the newsletter *The Intermarket Review*, and one of today's most influential thought leaders in the world of technical analysis. The author of McGraw-Hill's Martin Pring on Technical Analysis series, Pring has written more than a dozen trading books and has contributed to *Barron's* and other national publications. He was awarded the Jack Frost Memorial Award from the Canadian Technical Analysts Society.